IDEAS OF THE
GREAT PHILOSOPHERS

EVERYDAY HANDBOOKS

IDEAS OF THE GREAT PHILOSOPHERS

WILLIAM S. SAHAKIAN, Ph.D.
Chairman, Department of Philosophy
Suffolk University

MABEL LEWIS SAHAKIAN, D.Sc.
Lecturer in Philosophy
Northeastern University

BARNES & NOBLE BOOKS
A DIVISION OF HARPER & ROW, PUBLISHERS
New York, Hagerstown, San Francisco, London

L. C. catalogue card number: 66-23155

SBN 389 00256 9

87 88 89 90   20 19 18 17 16 15 14

Manufactured in the United States of America

Dedicated to all young men
of high potential
who lost their lives in World War II
but especially to the memory
of
Clyde Royden Sample
and
Paul Tyson Lewis, Jr.

PREFACE

Philosophy, technically defined, is the *critical evaluation* of all the facts of experience. In this definition, the term *critical* implies that the philosopher must view all data and propositions with searching scrutiny, rejecting bias or prejudice of any kind. But the key term which most accurately indicates the philosopher's task is *evaluation;* the philosopher evaluates all the facts of experience known to man, whereas the scientist merely *describes* selected facts of experience which lie within his special field. Consequently, it is the act of evaluation which distinguishes philosophy from the other disciplines.

The political scientist, for example, describes the operations of government as they in fact exist, but the philosopher evaluates them with a view to determining the best or ideal form of government. Similarly, the psychologist describes human behavior, but the philosopher evaluates it in order to differentiate good from evil behavior, a life worth living from one which is not worth while.

The five principal areas of philosophy discussed in the present work are as follows: Epistemology and Logic; Ethics and Philosophies of Life; Political and Legal Philosophy; the Philosophy of Religion; and Metaphysics. The concluding section (Part Six) briefly summarizes the major types (or schools) of philosophy. Thoughtful reading of the six Parts will provide a view of the nature and scope of philosophy and will enable the reader to delve further into any area of greatest concern to him. Each Part can be read independently, however, in accordance with the reader's interest and preference.

W.S.S.
M.L.S.

CONTENTS

PREFACE   vii

PART ONE—EPISTEMOLOGY AND LOGIC   3
Criteria of Truth   3
Material Fallacies of Reasoning   11
The Problem of Truth   23

PART TWO—ETHICS AND PHILOSOPHIES OF LIFE   31
The Philosophy of Socrates   32
The Self-Realization Philosophy of Aristotle   33
The Hedonistic Philosophy of Epicurus   37
The Stoic Philosophy of Epictetus   38
The Utilitarian Philosophy of Jeremy Bentham   41
The Utilitarianism of John Stuart Mill   43
The Intuitionism of Immanuel Kant   45
The Pessimistic Philosophy of Arthur Schopenhauer   48
The Naturalistic Philosophy of Friedrich Nietzsche   50
Royce's Philosophy of Loyalty   52
The Ethical Realism of George Edward Moore   53

PART THREE—SOCIAL, POLITICAL, AND LEGAL
PHILOSOPHY   59
Plato's Republic   59
The Political Philosophy of Aristotle   62
The Legal Philosophy of Saint Thomas Aquinas   65
Machiavelli's Political Philosophy   68
The Political Philosophy of Thomas Hobbes   69
The Democratic Philosophy of Jean Jacques Rousseau   73
Hegel's Philosophy of Law   75
The Communism of Karl Marx   78

PART FOUR—PHILOSOPHY OF RELIGION 85
Conceptions of God 86
The Problem of God's Existence 92
Agnosticism and Atheism 100
The Soul 104
The Mind-Body Problem 105
Immortality 108
The Problem of Evil 113

PART FIVE—METAPHYSICS 119
Pre-Cartesian Metaphysics 121
Modern Post-Cartesian Metaphysics 128

PART SIX—TYPES OF PHILOSOPHY 147
Dialectical Materialism 147
Pragmatism and Instrumentalism 150
Classical Positivism 153
Logical Positivism and the Analytic School 154
Neo-Scholasticism and Neo-Thomism 156
Neorealism and Critical Realism 160
Personalism 163
Phenomenology and Phenomenalism 165
Existentialism and Neo-Orthodoxy 167

INDEX 171

PART ONE—EPISTEMOLOGY
AND LOGIC

PART ONE—EPISTEMOLOGY AND LOGIC

Epistemology is that branch of philosophy treating the scope and limits of knowledge. It seeks to resolve basic questions such as: What is the nature of knowledge? How much can a human being know? Is knowledge possible? What are the practical and theoretical limitations of knowledge? (The term *epistemology* is from the Greek, signifying the study of knowledge.)

Logic may be regarded as a subdivision of epistemology. The principal task of logic is to investigate the nature of correct thinking and valid reasoning, including the laws of rational thought.

To explore the entire scope of epistemology and logic would require many volumes and a lifetime of study. In this part, however, the reader will find helpful summaries of some of the main problems and several approaches to their solution. The discussion will consider the criteria used to distinguish between truth and error, an analysis of the major fallacies of reasoning, and, finally, the central problem of the nature of truth itself, including the question whether or not truth is attainable.

CRITERIA OF TRUTH

One important area of logic is concerned with tests of truth —the criteria used to distinguish truth from error. A criterion of truth is a standard, or rule, by which to judge the accuracy of statements and opinions; thus, it is a standard of verification.

To obtain a clear, correct view of any philosophy, one must understand its criteria of truth. This is particularly the case because of the many conflicting ideas to be found in different philosophies. The laws of logic cannot of themselves disclose facts about the world of man or nature. In order to discover such facts, or to evaluate the content of an argument, the individual

3

must decide upon the criteria which can enable him to distinguish what is true from what is not true.

Not all criteria have equal validity or value; while some are adequate, others are of questionable worth. The criteria dealt with in the present discussion have been chosen, not necessarily because they may be widely regarded as most useful or adequate but rather because they have become most familiar to, and are in common use among, the general public and academic or scholarly circles.

Custom.   Many persons either knowingly or unwittingly employ custom as a criterion of truth, assuming that doing what is customary will not lead them too far astray. The admonition, "When in Rome, do as the Romans do," expresses an appeal to custom as a criterion, particularly in matters involving the determination of moral truth. Thus people adhere closely to custom as a criterion when they dress as others dress, use expressions which are in vogue, practice moral principles currently approved —in other words, do whatever is popular.

Custom scarcely merits serious consideration as a criterion of truth. Surely, a scientist obtaining evidence of facts or principles could never accept conflicting customs of majorities, or of minorities either, as a test. A public opinion poll can never be the best way to determine scientific truths.

Tradition.   Closely allied to custom as a proposed test of truth is tradition, the notion that what lasts for generations must be valid. Those who accept tradition as a criterion may defend their view on the ground that any practice which has gained the loyalty of succeeding generations must deserve a measure of credibility.

The same objections to custom as a standard of truth apply to tradition as well. Many traditions merely repeat what is false (consider, for example, the innumerable false traditions of primitive tribes) and, moreover, traditions often conflict with one another. It is clear that science cannot accept tradition as its test of truth.

Time.   Perhaps you have heard some person in a debate appeal to time as the test of truth, arguing with statements such as, "My belief has stood the test of time," or "Christianity must be true, for it has stood the test of time." The logic of such argument is based on the assumption that if a belief is really erroneous, the error will sooner or later come to light, whereas, if there is nothing wrong with the belief, the mere passage of time cannot destroy its validity.

Time is not an adequate test of truth. It is closely related to custom and tradition, which, in fact, are simply aspects of the time factor. The inadequacy of time as a criterion becomes apparent if we note that many errors have lasted for a very long time before being exposed as errors. The most absurd superstitions have endured throughout generations, centuries, even millenia. Surely, modern peoples who believe in the truth of a great religion, such as Christianity, would not give up their beliefs and change to some other system of religion which happened to be hundreds or perhaps thousands of years older than their own religion.

Feelings (Emotions).   Many individuals faced with the necessity of making a decision allow their emotions to sway them despite contrary evidence or without even attempting to obtain and evaluate evidence. Such people are implicitly accepting emotions as a test of truth. Too many depend upon subjective feelings as a guide to a great variety of situations, ranging from trivial problems of everyday living to the most serious problems of the community.

Most people today, however, will admit that they cannot trust their emotions in important matters. Thus the experienced business executive ignores his feelings and searches for facts when making investments. The scientist, physician, historian, and scholars in other fields have similarly learned to ignore subjective reactions of this kind.

Instinct.   The existence of separate instincts has long been in dispute. Instinctive behavior may be regarded as akin to feeling, or perhaps as a universal mode of feeling. From this point of view, it is the instinct of thirst that impels us to drink, the instinct of hunger to eat, etc. Some have gone so far as to assert that even the existence of God can be proved by reference to instinct, arguing that all instincts have their corresponding objects in the world of reality. Thus the corresponding object for the thirst instinct is a liquid; for the hunger instinct, food; for the sex instinct, a mate. The argument therefore concludes that, since all persons are religious, religion must be an instinct and its counterpart, God, must exist.

Instincts cannot be accepted as reliable tests: too often they are vague, ill-defined, variant and undependable, limited to specific types of activity. Even if we did accept instincts as valid tests, they are so few that we could not derive much evidence from them. To what extent could a scientist refer to them in his efforts to determine the composition of chemical substances?

Hunch.   A hunch is an impulsive generalization, perhaps based on a vague or undefined notion. It can hardly be regarded as an acceptable criterion of truth, yet many persons confronted with a choice may allow a hunch to be the decisive factor. Hunches are closely related both to feeling and to intuition, another criterion discussed below.

Intuition.   This criterion consists of judgment without recourse to reasoning from facts; it is an assumed truth issuing from an unknown or unexplored source. Many persons gain intuitive insights which later prove to be true. Some scientists, without employing the rational cognitive processes of the mind, hit upon a useful hypothesis or proof while merely resting, daydreaming, or doing other things which have no apparent relationship to the truths they are seeking to discover.

Intuition as a criterion of truth suffers from two major objections: (1) It is not available when needed; it cannot be depended upon in given situations in the same or at least similar manner that reason may be employed. (2) Intuitions are, at best, potential sources of truth, not tests; when a person claims to have an intuition, he should immediately test it in order to determine whether it is true or false.

Revelation.   The main difference between intuition and revelation is the fact that the source of intuition is unknown, whereas the source of revelation is assumed to be God. Revelation may be defined as a truth or disclosure which emanates from God. Many religions rely heavily upon the validity of revelation as a criterion of truth.

The adverse criticism stated above in regard to intuition holds good for revelation as well. When a person possesses what he claims to be a revelation, it is incumbent upon him to prove it, and the standard to which he appeals as the test consequently becomes his criterion. An individual may accept revelation as a source of some truths, but he cannot depend on such experience as a means of demonstrating to others the validity of his beliefs.

Majority Rule. The criterion of majority rule is a statistical basis for the acceptance of assertions or proposals. In democratic countries and organizations, majority vote is accepted by all members of a group as a guide to joint decisions. This is particularly true during enactment of laws pertaining to personal morality and social behavior. Often, however, a democratic community, divided into several opposing factions, must be content with a mere plurality.

Although a majority vote is good democratic procedure, it is not the best system for determining truth. Think what would happen if a scientist tried to arrive at conclusions by means of a majority vote—if, for example, an astronomer took a vote among the general population to ascertain whether assertions about the planets or stars were to be accepted as true or rejected as false.

Consensus Gentium. There are those who believe that the opinions held in common by all people comprise an acceptable criterion of truth. *Consensus gentium*, the unanimous opinion of mankind (universal or general consent), is believed to have a validity which is not to be found in majority decisions. According to this criterion, the fact that all human beings adhere to a given belief proves it to be necessarily true.

There is some cogency in *consensus gentium* if it means a universal innate truth such as the principles of logic and mathematics, but if it means merely general assent, as reflected by a unanimous vote cast in favor of a given decision, its value is questionable. General assent proves little—thus, at one time the masses believed that the world was flat and that the sun revolved about the earth.

Naive Realism. According to Naive Realism, things are in reality as the senses depict them. Human sense organs determine the truth or falsity of objects and conclusions. Only that which is subject to first-hand observation is verifiable. The expression, "I'm from Missouri, I have to be shown," exemplifies this criterion, the idea being, "Unless I see it, I will not believe it."

Naive Realism is an inadequate criterion of truth; for example, scientific truths are often beyond the scope of the senses. X rays, light waves, chemical reactions, and a host of other natural phenomena cannot be sensed, though they are understood and demonstrably real. Naive Realism as a valid test of truth would impel us to conclude that a straight stick in water is actually bent because it appears bent to our sense of vision. Sounds with a wave frequency above 20,000 cycles per second can be detected indirectly even though man's auditory sense does not reveal them. Furthermore, sense experience can be quite illusory; for instance, six pencil points touching a person's small of the back (remaining within the two-point threshold) are sensed as only one and Naive Realism would compel us to conclude erroneously that this sense experience is correct.

Correspondence. The criterion of correspondence states that an idea which agrees with its object is necessarily true. Thus the statement that the White House is situated in Washington, D.C., is true if the fact as to its location corresponds with the idea in the statement.

Correspondence appears to be the best of the criteria presented above—and many philosophers consider it to be the most valid of all tests of truth—but, like the rest, this criterion is subject to adverse criticism. Granted, an idea which corresponds to its object is indeed true, but how can one determine whether or not his idea does in fact bear a perfect correspondence to its object? To make this determination requires the use of some criterion other than correspondence. But if another test of truth has to be applied, the correspondence criterion becomes merely a *definition* of truth, not a decisive *test*. In other words, besides asserting correspondence between an idea and reality, we still need to apply a test that will disclose the precise degree of similarity between what we think and what actually exists.

Authority. Often the opinions of highly trained men who have achieved a degree of success in a given area of specialization are regarded as acceptable evidence or proof. These specialists, or authorities, can be relied upon because of their acquaintance with and mastery of a particular subject. They are admittedly capable of reasoning with accuracy in matters in which they are regarded as expert; consequently, their proposals command respect and their statements are accepted as criteria of truth. However, a person cannot merely pose as an authority in an *ipse dixit* (I myself said so) manner, but must be duly qualified.

Although authority is often a particularly good criterion of truth—one that is widely and effectively used (e.g., in a court of law)—this criterion is far from being final, for in many instances two noted authorities may give contradictory evidence.

The Pragmatic Criterion of Truth. To the Pragmatist, if an idea works, it must be accepted as true. In other words, the workability of an idea determines its truth. From the consequences which issue from a given idea, its truth is obtained or measured. Since ideas produce results, examination of the results will either verify or disprove the ideas themselves. The full meaning of an idea is to be found in the consequences which follow from its application; thus, the results of the administration of penicillin to cure bacterial infection will prove the validity and disclose the significance of the statement that the drug is an effective therapeutic agent.

Although Pragmatism offers a most valuable criterion of truth, the criterion must be viewed with reservations and used with caution. Not all ideas that appear to be working are true; for example, a physician who apparently cures a patient's neurosis by prescribing a given medicine and accepts it as a remedy may later discover that the use of a placebo (innocuous medication) which resembles the original medicine works equally well. He may be compelled to admit that the medication was not effective and that his initial judgment was incorrect. (Perhaps psychic experience or faith effected the cure.) Such instances indicate that untrue ideas may seem to be working in practice contrary to the pragmatic test.

Nevertheless, there is definite validity in Pragmatism as a criterion, at least that kind of validity characterized (by William Ernest Hocking) as Negative Pragmatism. In brief, this principle states that, if an idea does not work, then it cannot possibly be true, for the reason that the truth always works (even though at times what appears to be working may or may not be true).

Loose (or Mere) Consistency.   Correct, but not necessarily related, statements are said to be consistent if they do not contradict one another. (Similarly, an individual is consistent in so far as he does not contradict himself.) Thus, consistency is attributed to the following statements because none of them negates any of the others: "Snow is white." "A ton of lead is heavy." "Yesterday the temperature dropped to twenty degrees." "George Washington was the first president of the United States."

The inadequacy of loose consistency as a criterion of truth is readily detected because the consistent statements are disconnected and lack cohesiveness or integration. The value of proof lies in its relationships which integrate isolated data into a coherent whole.

Rigorous Consistency.   The criterion of rigorous consistency refers to connections between statements such that one proposition follows necessarily from another. Mathematical and formal logical reasoning exemplify this criterion. Examples are: "If all generals in the U.S. Army are also soldiers, and if John Doe is a general in the U.S. Army, then it follows necessarily that John Doe is a soldier." "If all A's are B's and all B's are C's, then all A's are C's."

The value of rigorous consistency is to be granted; however, the areas to which this form of reasoning is applicable are limited. Furthermore, the premises are taken for granted; that is to say, to establish their accuracy requires another criterion of truth.

A further objection states that despite rigorous consistency, a set of philosophical conclusions may display lack of coherence. Moreover, a system of philosophy may be rigorously consistent with only those facts which it has included for consideration, whereas an adequate criterion must take all facts into consideration, whether or not the new data are detrimental to the system in question.

Coherence.   As a criterion of truth, coherence refers to a systematic consistent explanation of all the facts of experience. To be coherent, a person must arrange all pertinent facts so that they will be in proper relationship to one another consistently and cohesively as parts of an integrated whole. Whatever facts are brought to light must be explained, must somehow be fitted into the system as a relevant or integral part. That explanation which most fulfills the requirements of coherence may be regarded as adequately verified.

Of all the criteria treated, coherence meets the demands of a standard of verification or test of truth most adequately. It includes reason, facts, system, integration, relationships, consistency. Its obvious limitation lies not in the criterion of coherence, but in man's limitations or his inability to obtain *all* facts of experience. Only an omniscient mind possesses all facts of experience; consequently, man must be content to deal with all facts at his disposal at the present time, allowing that point to be regarded as proved true which is the most coherent under prevailing circumstances. That person, school of thought, or idea which is supported in a coherent manner by most of the facts must be accepted as verified.

One who objects to coherence as a criterion places himself in a delicate position logically, for he thus implies a preference for incoherence, which is absurd; furthermore, to attack coherence necessitates the use of a criterion that is either coherent and rational, or incoherent and irrational; to appeal to irrationality is absurd, thus obligating a person to accept coherence as his criterion of truth.

Finally, a moot question arises as to whether or not there could be several equally coherent systems, each containing all the facts of human experience.

MATERIAL FALLACIES OF REASONING

A second major realm of logic treats material fallacies, that is, erroneous ways of reasoning about facts. Material fallacies are numerous, deceptive, and elusive—so elusive that a person untrained in detecting them can easily be misled into accepting them as valid. Not only logicians but also careful scientists and other competent scholars are especially adept at detecting and avoiding fallacies; their knowledge of logic is particularly refined. In fact, the necessity of reasoning without committing error is an obvious asset for all persons, regardless of their walk in life.

The fallacies which concern us here are all properly classified as *material* (that is, the error lies in the factual content of the argument rather than in the structure of it), yet it may prove helpful to subdivide them in some manner. Accordingly, the following subclassification will be used: (1) *linguistic fallacies,* or those which involve the abuse or misuse of language, a play on words; (2) *fallacies of irrelevant evidence,* or arguments which miss the central point at issue and rely principally upon emotions, feelings, ignorance, etc., to defend a thesis (some logicians consider these a manner of debate, a type of argument, rather than fallacies); (3) miscellaneous fallacies which belong to a number of other classifications but which do not readily lend themselves to further subdivision.

Occasionally, fallacies will be found to overlap, which is understandable, particularly when one realizes that they belong to interrelated families. Furthermore, an argument may contain a number of fallacies, but not all will be equally crucial in destroying the validity of an argument. One must detect the decisive error, distinguishing it from the rest, yet be alert to the possibility of additional fallacies present in the argument.

Linguistic Fallacies.   These fallacies include those of emotive language; ambiguity; equivocation; amphibology; speech; composition; division; and vicious abstraction.

FALLACY OF EMOTIVE LANGUAGE.   Often words used in arguments either lack definite meaning or have as their sole purpose the arousal of unreasoned feeling; when an argument depends upon the stimulation of emotions rather than conveying logical information, the error committed is known as the fallacy of emotive language.

For example, in the United States, the purpose of labeling someone a *Communist* is not usually to convey the thought that he believes in the "common ownership of the means of production," but to insult him, to cast a derogatory aspersion upon him, to refer to him with contempt.

FALLACY OF AMBIGUITY.   Occasionally a person takes refuge in language; that is, he hides behind words which lack precise meaning, or words whose definition is unknown either to one or to both parties in a discussion. The fallacy of ambiguity refers to the use of terms which are ill-defined, vague in meaning, signifying a variety of ideas, none of which can be made clear or precise either by definition of the words or by the context. Some logicians regard all linguistic fallacies as aspects of the error of ambiguity.

FALLACY OF EQUIVOCATION. The use of a term in more than one sense, while the impression is given that it is being used to express only one and the same meaning throughout an argument, is known as the fallacy of equivocation. A word used in more than one sense should be interpreted as if it were actually two or more words; the fallacy results from the incorrect assumption that the word is used throughout a given discussion to convey a single connotation.

For example, in the following argument, the word "adjective" is responsible for the fallacy of equivocation:

"The United States is large. Large is an adjective. Therefore, the United States is an adjective."

The misused word in the example below is "radioactive":

"It is dangerous for people to touch that which is radioactive. The word used here is 'radioactive.' Therefore, people should not touch the word used here."

FALLACY OF AMPHIBOLOGY. The use of a statement which permits of two interpretations is known as the fallacy of amphibology. Amphibology differs from equivocation in two important respects: (1) amphibology pertains to the entire argument, whereas equivocation is limited to single terms; (2) the entire argument is susceptible to a two-fold interpretation due to its structure, not to any misuse on the part of the debater. As in the following examples, amphibologies are often attributable to the use of misplaced modifiers:

"The duke yet lives that Henry shall depose." (In this sentence from Shakespeare's *Henry VI*, who is deposing whom? Henry, the duke; or the duke, Henry?)

"Wanted to sell: A highchair for a baby with a broken leg." (In this classified advertisement, which is broken, the chair or the child's leg?)

"Clean and decent boxing every night except Sunday." (According to this sign at a boxing arena, what happens on Sundays —no boxing whatever, or dirty and indecent boxing?)

FIGURE OF SPEECH FALLACY. Failure to distinguish between variant meanings of sentence elements, such as suffixes, may give rise to the figure of speech fallacy. This fallacy is more common in certain foreign languages (Greek is a good example) than it is in English. (Aristotle, initially responsible for identifying this fallacy, encountered it in his native Greek.) John Stuart Mill, one of the most careful logicians of the nineteenth century was, nevertheless, guilty of the figure of speech fallacy in the following statements: "The only proof capable of being given that an object is visible, is that people actually see it. The only proof that a sound is audible, is that people hear it; and so of the other sources of our experience. In like manner, I apprehend, the sole evidence it is possible to produce that anything is desirable, is that people do actually desire it." [1]

Mill's error lies in assuming that the suffix *ble* conveys the same meaning in each instance. It is true that "visible" means "can be seen" and "audible" means "can be heard"; however, "desirable" does *not* mean "can be desired" but merely "ought to be desired." To say that the removal of a tumor is desirable does not signify that the individual will actually desire it, but that it ought to be desired, whereas to say that thunder is audible means that it can be heard and under favorable circumstances actually is heard.

FALLACY OF COMPOSITION. The false assumption that a statement about an integral part of something necessarily holds true for the composite whole is known as the fallacy of composition. This error refers to statements about things considered as parts of a whole, not to statements about things considered as separate entities. The fallacy consists of reasoning incorrectly from facts about members of a class to conclusions about the entire class. Often the whole is a *Gestalt,* greater than the sum of its parts, an organic whole which does not have a one-to-one relationship to its parts. (Some logicians, such as Jevons, consider the fallacy

---

[1] John Stuart Mill, *Utilitarianism* (London, 1863; 12th ed., 1895).

of composition to be a special form of equivocation, involving confusion of an isolated part with the collective whole.)

Note these examples of the fallacy of composition: "A Hollywood film production composed exclusively of top stars would be a better show than one composed of a few star actors." (The error lies in neglecting to note the need for a good supporting cast who have not attained stardom.) "An orchestra of the world's finest soloists would be the best band in the world." (An orchestra is a *team* of musicians, each lending proper support to the whole, not a mere assembly of individual prima donnas, each playing solos independently of the group effort.)

FALLACY OF DIVISION. The converse of the fallacy of composition is division, erroneous reasoning that what holds true of a composite whole necessarily is true for each component part considered separately. The whole, if it is an organic whole, a *Gestalt,* cannot be divided as a mathematical whole; you may divide a hundred into twos, but you cannot divide a flower similarly.

Note the following examples of this fallacy: "The New York Yankees were the world's champion baseball team last year; therefore, they must have had the world's best second baseman." (The second baseman may have been their weakest link; they may have become champions despite this weakness.) "California grows the world's best grapes; therefore, the Californian grape which I am about to eat must be one of the best in the world." (It may be a poor specimen or rotten grape.)

FALLACY OF VICIOUS ABSTRACTION. The removal of a statement from its context, thereby changing the meaning of an argument, is known as the fallacy of vicious abstraction. Many statements may easily and critically be altered simply by dropping the context; this emasculates the statement and distorts its meaning. Below are four examples of this fallacy, each followed by a corrected statement:

"St. Paul said, 'Money is the root of all evil.'" ("The *love* of money is the root of all evil.") "Ralph Waldo Emerson said: 'Consistency is the hobgobblin of little minds.'" ("*Foolish* consistency is the hobgobblin of little minds.") "Alexander Pope said, 'Learning is a dangerous thing.'" ("A *little* learning is a dangerous thing; drink deep, or taste not the Pierian spring. There shallow draughts intoxicate the brain, and drinking largely sobers us again.") "Francis Bacon said, 'Philosophy inclineth man's mind to atheism.'" ("A *little* philosophy inclineth man's mind to atheism, but depth in philosophy bringeth men's minds about to religion.")

Fallacies of Irrelevant Evidence.   Seven classes of these fallacies are listed below.

Fallacy of Irrelevance.   To prove or disprove the wrong point is to commit the fallacy of *irrelevance*, often referred to as *irrelevant conclusion* or *ignoratio elenchi*. The fallacy of irrelevance can be most deceptive, for the presentation may seem very cogent, obscuring the fact that a question different from the one under consideration is being discussed. Thus, instead of proving point *A*, which is at issue, the speaker proves unrelated point *B*; or instead of disproving point *C*, he disproves point *D*. This error is made by attempting to prove something that has not even been denied or by attacking something that has not been asserted. In another form of this fallacy, the individual assumes that he has proved his own point by disproving those of his opponent. In a murder trial, for example, a prosecutor is guilty of the fallacy of irrelevance if, instead of proving the defendant guilty of murder, he proves him to be guilty of other crimes.

Argumentum ad Ignorantiam (the Appeal to Ignorance). The fallacy of the appeal to ignorance takes several forms. In one form, it is assumed that what might possibly be true is actually true. In a second form, it is assumed that a given thesis is correct merely because no one can prove it to be incorrect. (Of course, the burden of proof should fall upon the individual who advances the thesis, not upon his opponent.) In a third form, it is assumed that an opponent's entire argument can be destroyed merely by disproving a nonessential part of the argument. The following are examples of the fallacy of the appeal to ignorance: "Psychic phenomena are facts, for no one can absolutely disprove them." "Flying saucers do exist, for no one really knows for sure that they don't."

Argumentum ad Misericordiam (the Appeal to Pity).   Instead of defending an argument on its merits, this fallacy evades the pertinent issues and makes a purely emotional appeal. Too often a person who is unable to cite relevant facts in support of his claims may resort to a plea for sympathy. (An attorney may be tempted to do this when he defends his client before a jury.) Nevertheless, some logicians insist that in certain instances the *argumentum ad misericordiam* is a legitimate argument.

The fallacy of the appeal to pity is illustrated in the following statements: "Teacher, I did not do my home assignment because my baby sister cried all night." (This might in some cases be accepted as a justifiable excuse.) "Teacher, please change my grade from C to B; if you do not, then I shall miss being on the honor roll, and consequently fail to attain scholarship assistance which I desperately need."

ARGUMENTUM AD VERECUNDIAM (THE APPEAL TO PRESTIGE). The appeal to respect or prestige (instead of to pertinent data) is known as *argumentum ad verecundiam*. This fallacy equates prestige with evidence. The attempt is made to gain support for an idea or proposal by associating it with highly respected individuals or hallowed institutions. (It is true that deserving men and institutions should be esteemed, but their approval of a thesis must not be used in lieu of evidence. (The same type of incorrect reasoning may encourage excessive faith in authority, discussed as a criterion of truth on p. 8.) Note the dubious appeals in the following arguments: "I have a wonderful idea which you should accept because I learned it from a seminar at Oxford University." "Son, listen to what I have to say, and please do not contradict, but respect your elders."

ARGUMENTUM AD BACULUM (THE APPEAL TO FORCE). An appeal to force (whether the coercion be overt or disguised) as a substitute for pertinent logic is known as *argumentum ad baculum* (argument by means of a club), the idea being that a club held over an opponent's head will force him to accept a new point of view.

This fallacy is evident in the following statement: "Mr. Jones, we like only intelligent men in our organization; if you do not want to lose your job, then I suggest that you show a little intelligence by taking part in civic activities—e.g., by supporting my brother's campaign for election to the school committee." In another example, when a boy tells his father, "Dad, I don't believe in altruism," his father replies, "You had better, or I will not give you a present for your birthday."

ARGUMENTUM AD HOMINEM (APPEAL TO PERSONAL RIDICULE). The fallacy of shifting an argument from the point being discussed to the personality of an opponent is known as *argumentum ad hominem*. Instead of dealing with an opponent's thesis on its merits, the fallacious argument attacks his reputation and moral character, or refers to his low intelligence, inferior social position, lack of education, or similar personal shortcomings. (The fallacy is illustrated by statements such as: "Don't stoop to debate with this man, for he is nothing but an ignorant savage." "That candidate would never make a good president, for he is divorced from his wife." "I don't care what the proof indicates. Would you accept evidence presented by this low contemptible heathen?")

ARGUMENTUM AD POPULUM (APPEAL TO THE MASSES). Arguments which depart from the question under discussion by making an appeal to the feelings and prejudices of the multitude are known as *ad populum* fallacies. These arguments often take the affirmative form of an appeal to patriotism, or they may consist of negative appeals to superiority feelings and racial or religious prejudices. Hitler's Nazis and Mussolini's Fascists used these fallacies as a basic technique of their propaganda, coupling the appeal with promises of wealth and power for faithful adherents.

Miscellaneous Material Fallacies. In addition to the two preceding classes of fallacies, there are a number of miscellaneous fallacies not readily subject to classification, of which the following are commonly encountered.

FALLACY OF ACCIDENT (OR DICTO SIMPLICITER). This fallacy attempts to apply a general rule to special cases which are exceptions to the rule, that is, to make universal statements about matters to which the rule does not always apply. It is an error to ignore the fact that most rules permit of exceptions. Furthermore, a rule may be valid only if certain conditions prevail, and different conditions may make the rule inapplicable to specific cases. This fallacy is illustrated by statements, such as the following: "Theft is a crime. Since the Spartan nation permitted stealing, it must have consisted entirely of criminals." (Theft is a crime only in those nations in which it is prohibited by law; wherever not prohibited, it is of course legally permissible, as in ancient Sparta. True, nations generally regard theft as criminal, but to apply this common view to an exception, as in the case of Sparta, is to commit the fallacy of accident.)

CONVERSE FALLACY OF ACCIDENT. This fallacy, also called the fallacy of *selected instances* or the fallacy of *hasty generalization*, consists of an attempt to establish a generalization (rule or scientific law) by the simple enumeration of instances without obtaining a representative number of particular instances. In other words, a conclusion is derived before all the particular instances have been taken into consideration. Examples of this fallacy follow: "All geniuses are odd people. I know, because the first five geniuses I interviewed were strangely peculiar." (The error lies in failing to obtain a fair or representative sampling of geniuses.) "Professors are absentminded." (Obviously, this trait displayed by a few professors must not be attributed to the entire profession.)

FALSE CAUSE (POST HOC). The fallacy of *false cause*, or *post hoc*, consists of reasoning from mere sequence to consequence, that is, from what merely happened in sequence to the assumption of a causal connection. The fact that *A* precedes *B*, does not necessarily make *A* the cause of *B*. The basic error is that of inferring a causal relationship without sufficient grounds; for this reason the fallacy is often referred to as that of *post hoc ergo propter hoc* (after this and therefore in consequence of this), an expression which itself explains the nature of the error. Note the following examples: "Twice in succession John raised his hand, and lightning flashed; therefore, the raising of John's hand causes lightning." (It was of course a coincidence that lightning occurred simultaneously with John's action.) "Mary said, 'When I remember to knock on wood, then I never become ill; therefore, knocking on wood prevents illness.'"

NON SEQUITUR (IT DOES NOT FOLLOW)—or Fallacy of the Consequent. A *non sequitur* consists of an acceptance of a conclusion which does not follow logically from given premises or from any antecedent statements. A non sequitur argument always exhibits this lack of a logical connection. The difference between the *post hoc* and the *non sequitur* fallacies is that, whereas the *post hoc* fallacy is due to lack of a causal connection, in the *non sequitur* fallacy, the error is due to lack of a logical connection. A *non sequitur* argument should also be distinguished from an irrelevant inference, in which the statement being made pertains to a question other than the one up for discussion. In a *non sequitur* argument the statements may all be relevant, but the relationships posited are logically disconnected. Examples of non sequitur statements are: "Trees are green; therefore human beings enjoy spinach." "A high I.Q. is the sign of an intelligent person; therefore beautiful girls have a preference for the acting profession." "If it takes a man twenty minutes to walk a mile, women should be able to live longer than men."

COMPOUND QUESTIONS.   This fallacy is also known as the fallacy of *multiple questions,* or of *poisoning the wells.* The error consists of combining several questions in such a manner as to preclude all opposing arguments, thus placing one's opponent in a self-incriminating position. We can be misled into assuming that a simple, single question has been asked, whereas the wording of the question implies that prior questions have been raised and correctly answered as a basis for the question under consideration. Note the implied assumptions in the following questions: "Why did you torture this innocent child?" "Where did you hide the knife after you committed the murder?" "Have you stopped beating your wife?" "How do you account for your stupidity?" "Why am I always right, while you are always wrong?" "Why did you cheat your best friend?" (Some unethical attorneys have been known to use such misleading queries deliberately to trap a witness in a courtroom trial into making contradictory statements or to confuse him during cross-examination.)

PETITIO PRINCIPII (BEGGING THE QUESTION).   Perhaps no other fallacy has so many different names as *petitio principii,* which consists of several forms, such as reasoning in a circle, failing to prove the initial thesis propounded, and using the original thesis as proof of itself. Common terms for this fallacy are *circular reasoning, circle in the proof,* and *arguing in a circle.* In order to prove that *A* is true, *B* is used as proof, but since *B* requires support, *C* is used in defense of *B*, but *C* also requires proof and is substantiated by *A*, the proposition which was to be proved in the first place. Thus we see that what was to be proved in the first place is offered ultimately in defense of itself. Reasoning becomes completely circular, so that the initial question is begged.

"Gentlemen prefer blondes." "How do I know?" "A gentleman told me so." "How do you know he is a gentleman?" "I know for the simple reason that he prefers blondes." "Books on religion are better than books on atheism." "How do you know that?" "The experts all concur that religious books are better than atheistic ones." "Who are the experts?" "They are the ones who maintain that religious books are better than atheistic ones."

Tu Quoque (You Yourself Do It). Often an individual who is being criticized will defend his actions by accusing his critic of doing the same things himself. But what is sauce for the goose may not always be sauce for the gander. If the conditions are identical, this *tu quoque* argument can be used as an effective defense, but it is fallacious if the two situations being compared are not identical or if the actions of both parties are considered indefensible.

This fallacy is shown in discussions such as the following:

"If a heart specialist can lie to his patient, then I have the right to lie to my teacher." (The difference in motive is wrongly ignored.)

"Son, it is your bedtime. Go to bed." "But dad, you are staying up; therefore I should be allowed to do likewise." (The fact that the boy requires more sleep than his father does has been disregarded.)

Fallacy of Misplaced Authority. The discussion of authority as a source or criterion of truth suggested that any expert's opinion merits confidence and respect if it relates to his special field of competence. It is an error (the fallacy of misplaced authority) to cite an authority in matters foreign to his field of specialization. His opinion in matters beyond the scope of his area of acknowledged competence need be accorded no greater respect or attention than that of any other observer. The scientific opinions of a Newton or of an Einstein inspire confidence, but their political, religious, or artistic opinions must be judged on their merits in the same way as those of ordinary citizens. It would be indeed illogical and risky to depend upon the world's foremost mathematician instead of experienced physicians for medical decisions and treatment.

GENETIC ERROR. The genetic error confuses the validity with the causes or origins of a thesis. It is a mistake to assume that an argument is necessarily false merely because it can be traced back to humble beginnings in superstition, ignorance, and magic. The source of an argument is irrelevant so far as logical proof or disproof is concerned. The statements that 5 and 5 are 10 and that carbon monoxide is a poison remain true and logically valid whether made by an insane person or by a normal individual.

FALSE ANALOGY. Arguments which resemble each other in logical reasoning are said to be analogous. If one argument is accepted as valid, then the others involving the same line of reasoning are also accepted. But any major differences between propositions may destroy the analogy and vitiate the conclusions. Note the false analogy in the following statement: "Women should make better congressmen than men, for government is merely good housekeeping." (The analogy is false because there are major differences between administration of government affairs and management of a household.)

INSUFFICIENT EVIDENCE. The fallacy known as *insufficient evidence* refers to the acceptance of inadequate data as a basis for a conclusion. For example, in a trial for murder, the judge may remind the jury that evidence proving that the murder weapon belonged to the defendant does not in itself prove that he used it to commit the crime.

PATHETIC FALLACY (ANTHROPOMORPHISM). The pathetic fallacy ascribes human feelings and qualities to nonhuman animals or to inanimate objects. It is true that some characteristics are common to man and to other animals, but the distinctive traits of the human species should not be attributed to nonhuman entities—as, for example, in the following statement: "The mad sea looked angrily at the sky." (Obviously the sea cannot look anywhere, nor can it be described as emotionally disturbed.)

CONTRARY TO FACT CONDITIONAL ERROR. This fallacy alters historical facts and then draws conclusions from them. But conclusions derived from false premises cannot be accepted as valid. Logical conclusions cannot be drawn from unhistorical suppositions, but only from data accepted as historically true. The fallacy is illustrated in statements such as the following: "If the South had won the Civil War, then slavery would abound in the North today." (Actually, no one can tell what might have happened; the historical facts would have determined the outcome.)

CONTRADICTORY PREMISES. Self-Contradictions are necessarily false; consequently, when an argument contains premises which contradict each other, no conclusion is possible. Any conclusion would involve the *fallacy of contradictory premises;* that is, it would constitute a *self-contradiction.* When contradictory premises are present in an argument, one premise cancels out the other. It is possible for one or the other of the two premises to be true, but not for both to be simultaneously true. Note the contradictory premises in the following questions: "If God is all-powerful, can he put himself out of existence, then come to life with twice the power he had originally?" "Can God make a stone so heavy that he cannot lift it?" "Can God make a round square?" "What would happen if an irresistible force met an immovable object?" (One student's answer: "An inconceivable smash!")

THE PROBLEM OF TRUTH

From the earliest times, man has been haunted by the many-sided problem of truth. He has often attempted to formulate a definition of truth. He has speculated concerning the general nature of truth. Three major interpretations have emerged: (1) truth as absolute; (2) truth as subjective—as a matter of personal opinion; (3) truth as an unattainable entity, an impossibility.

DEFINITIONS OF TRUTH

The attempt to define truth involves a number of difficulties. For example, it is difficult to avoid projection of one's philosophical position into any definition. One's philosophical bias will inevitably be reflected; thus, the Existentialist *Martin Heidegger* would equate truth with freedom; *William James,* with relationships in terms of consequences; *Hegel,* with fully realized results;

Alfred Tarski, with a semantic concept; *George E. Moore,* with correspondence between appearance and reality; and *Aristotle,* with an adequate relationship between concept and object.

As a basis for this discussion, let us agree that *truth is a judgment which accords with reality,* that *our knowledge of reality and the fact of reality harmoniously conform,* that the integrated systems of *ideas which we have in mind correspond in exact detail with the world of reality.* We shall later consider to what extent it is possible to discover truth as here defined. At this point, let us review briefly the principal theories of various schools of philosophy concerning the nature of truth.

CONCEPTIONS OF TRUTH

The preceding definition of truth conforms in most respects to the adequation and correspondence theories developed by great philosophers, beginning with Aristotle and continuing through the Middle Ages and into contemporary philosophy. In modern times, other theories have been developed, such as the coherence, pragmatic, semantic, and existential theories. Aristotle and the Scholastics (particularly Saint Thomas Aquinas) propounded the Adequation Theory of Truth as the belief that *truth is the adequation of thought to thing* (*adaequatio intellectus et rei*). The intellect of man discovers facts through which it acquires truth; thus when man's ideas correspond to things as they exist, they reveal truth. "Truth is the adequation of the immanence in act of our thought with that which exists outside our thought." [1] Actually, truth resides in the intellect, but not only there, for it also resides in things. Consequently, the Adequation Theory may be regarded as a form of the Correspondence Theory of Truth.

The Correspondence Theory of Truth. George E. Moore has ably expounded the Correspondence Theory of Truth, which defines *truth as the correspondence of ideas to reality.* If an idea corresponds with its counterpart in the world of reality, it is a true idea. The facts themselves are not true or false, but the

---

[1] Jacques Maritain, *Existence and the Existent* (New York: Pantheon Books, 1948).

beliefs are; truth and falsity are predicated of ideas, statements, and beliefs, which must possess a corresponding relationship to the facts which they mirror. Thus the common property of truth is its correspondence to fact; falsity lacks this property. Truth consists of those beliefs which picture (or are identified with) the elements and structure of the universe.

The Coherence Theory of Truth. This theory was first set forth in the philosophies of Benedict Spinoza and Georg Hegel (although crude beginnings can be found in pre-Socratic writings) and was accepted in various forms by later philosophers, such as Francis Herbert Bradley, Brand Blanshard, Edgar Sheffield Brightman, and Rudolf Carnap. These philosophers consider truth to be a coherent interrelated system or body of propositions. A statement is true if it can be incorporated in an orderly and consistent way within that corpus of propositions.

For Spinoza, ultimate reality (Substance or God) is a rational system, each aspect of which is necessarily related to the rest. For Hegel, "the truth is the whole," an integrated rational system, while falsity is abstraction, statements out of context, partials divorced from the systematic whole, hence incoherent. The fully realized result is the truth. For the British Neo-Hegelians, Blanshard, Bradley and Brightman, truth (as Hegel proposed) is an Absolute, an exhaustive and all-embracing whole, while falsity consists of fragments separated from the whole. Finally, Rudolf Carnap's Coherence Theory differs from the others in that he believes that a proposition is true if it coheres with an accepted theory or symbolic system.

The Pragmatic Theory of Truth. The Pragmatists maintain that a belief is true if it is worth committing us to action, and that only such a belief corresponds with reality. William James explained the pragmatic point of view as follows: "Pragmatism . . . asks its usual question. 'Grant an idea or belief to be true,' it says, 'what concrete difference will its being true make in any one's actual life? How will the truth be realized? What experiences will be different from those which would obtain if the belief were false? What, in short, is the truth's cash value in experiential terms?' The moment Pragmatism asks this question, it sees the answer: *True ideas are those that we can assimilate, vali-*

date, corroborate and verify. False ideas are those that we can not.
That is the practical difference it makes to us to have true ideas;
that, therefore, is the meaning of truth, for it is all that truth is
known as. . . . Truth *happen*s to an idea. It *becomes* true, is
made true by events." According to Pragmatists, then, truth is
particular, that is to say, there are many individual truths (instead of one integrated system of truth postulated by the coherence theory).

The Semantic Theory of Truth. In 1944 Alfred Tarski set
forth his semantic conception of truth in an article in the journal,
Philosophy and Phenomenological Research. Truth is predicated of sentences as a *meta-language* (a language which makes
symbolic assertions about another language). Truth is applicable
only to sentences, and is basically a semantic matter; that is,
*"it deals with certain relations between expressions of a language
and the objects 'referred to' by those expressions."*

The semantic idea of truth is closely related to the basic principles of theoretical semantics. The semantic definition has been
stated as follows: "All equivalences of the form (T) can be
asserted, and *we shall call a definition of truth 'adequate' if all
these equivalences follow from it.*" For example, we may predi-
cate true (T) to the sentence "snow is white," if and only if
"snow is white," that is, a material adequacy must exist between
the sentence and the fact, an equivalency between the sentence
and the existing state of affairs.

Existential Theory of Truth. The Existentialists, such as
Martin Heidegger, consider the essence of truth to be *freedom*.
Heidegger acknowledges value in other concepts of truth (truth
as reality, or as correspondence, or as an approximation to perception, or as an idea preconceived in the divine intellect),
but for him *"the essence of truth is freedom."*

By freedom is meant that "inner possibility of rightness" which
enables man to receive the "uniquely essential truth," a "revelation of something already overt." Truth is "unconcealment" or
"revealment," that is, the "participation in the revealed nature
of what-is." It is a "letting-be," a freedom "in its own self 'ex-
posing' and 'existent.' " Freedom is the "participation in the revealment of what-is-as such," the revelation of the existent (per-

son) participating in what is overtly there; "the 'there' (*Da*) of it, *is* what it is." Truth is basically a revelation of "what-is," and the essence of truth is freedom, a "participation in the revealment of what-is-in-totality." [1]

RELATIVITY VERSUS OBJECTIVITY OF TRUTH

Since the days of Socrates, debate has continued as to whether truth is *relative and subjective* or *absolute and objective*. Among the ancient Greeks, one school of thought, represented by Gorgias of Leontium (483-375 B.C.) went so far as to doubt that truth does in fact exist in any form. It has been said that there are no new truths but old ones, and, indeed, modern discussions concerning subjectivity of truth are no more than elaborations upon the ancient debates.

Truth as Relative. The most influential proponent of the concept of truth as relative was the sophist Protagoras of Abdera (481-411 B.C.). Protagoras based his conclusion on the fact that man's knowledge of the phenomenal world (the world which he senses) is imperfect owing to the imperfection of human senses. Not only do sensory defects of vision, hearing, etc. afflict most people, but even perfect sense equipment would be an inadequate basis for accurate perception of real objects. Instruments such as a magnifying glass or a microscope vastly increase the range of visual perception, while hearing devices can record sounds beyond the capacity of the human auditory apparatus. Obviously, man's sensory equipment is imperfect, limited, inadequate. It is assumed that human beings can therefore obtain only partial knowledge based upon partial experience, which differs from that which others obtain. Knowledge, at best, then, is opinion, a subjective truth. Since truth is opinion, what is true for me is true only for me, and what is true for you is true only for you.

Skepticism. Gorgias of Leontium carried Protagoras' point of view further by formulating a doctrine that is nihilistic (asserting that *truth does not exist*) and skeptical (asserting that *noth-*

---

[1] Martin Heidegger, *On the Essence of Truth,* tr. R. F. C. Hull and Alan Crick.

ing can be known). He put forth the threefold thesis (1) that nothing exists, (2) that, if anything did happen to exist, we could never know it, and (3) that, if by some accident man should come to know it, he would never be able to convey it to others.

Nihilism and Skepticism are both self-contradictory and self-defeating philosophies. If truth does not exist (Nihilism), then the posited truth of Nihilism could not exist. If knowledge is impossible (Skepticism), how could we ever come to know that? Apparently some things can be known.

Even the less extreme view of Protagoras is self-defeating, as demonstrated by Plato's charming argument in the following paragraphs.

Truth as Objective. From our discussion of Gorgias' negative view, it has become evident that the arguments of Nihilism and Skepticism can be used to destroy themselves. Note how the paraphrased dialogue below proves that Protagoras' Subjectivism is also self-defeating:

PROTAGORAS: Truth is relative, it is only a matter of opinion.

SOCRATES: You mean that truth is mere subjective opinion?

PROTAGORAS: Exactly. What is true for you is true for you, and what is true for me, is true for me. Truth is subjective.

SOCRATES: Do you really mean that? That my opinion is true by virtue of its being my opinion?

PROTAGORAS: Indeed I do.

SOCRATES: My opinion is: Truth is absolute, not opinion, and that you, Mr. Protagoras, are absolutely in error. Since this is my opinion, then you must grant that it is true according to your philosophy.

PROTAGORAS: You are quite correct, Socrates.

Obviously, any discussion concerning truth must begin on a positive footing, if it is to begin at all. The Relativist is expressing an absolute truth when he asserts that truth is not absolute, for he sincerely believes that the real truth (regardless of opinion) is that *truth is relative*. Hence he necessarily contradicts himself and implicitly admits that truth is objective, not relative.

PART TWO — ETHICS
AND PHILOSOPHIES OF LIFE

PART TWO—ETHICS
AND PHILOSOPHIES OF LIFE

The philosophical meaning of the term *ethics* is much broader than its narrow connotation in the parlance of the "man on the street," who restricts the meaning to a moral choice between right and wrong behavior. A major aspect of ethics, one which in the systems of many philosophers is more important than moral choice, deals with the *good life,* that is to say, the life worth living, the life that is satisfying. These philosophers consider the major problem to be the discovery of the *summum bonum,* life's greatest good. The right act can readily be known once the greatest good has been determined, for it becomes simply that act which enhances the realization of the greatest good, and the immoral act is that mode of behavior which is a deterrent to its realization. From this discussion one may conclude that ethics embodies two areas, namely, *right action* and life's *greatest good;* hence ethics may be defined as *the study of right conduct and the good life.*

Having defined the term *ethics* as the study of the right and the good, one must consider how it is related to other terms, such as *moral, immoral, unethical,* and *nonmoral.* The relationship between ethics and morals is like that between theory and practice, since the former denotes the *theory* of right conduct and the good life, whereas the latter refers to the actual *practice* of right conduct and the good life.

The term *moral* has a dual meaning: the first has to do with the ability of a person to understand morality as well as his capacity to make moral decisions; the second has to do with the actual performance of moral acts.

Using the term *moral* in the former sense, we may contrast it with *amoral,* which refers to a being incapable of distinguishing between right and wrong. Using the term *moral* in the latter sense, we may contrast it to *immoral,* which refers to actions which transgress moral principles. (The terms *nonmoral* and *unmoral* are often used interchangeably with *amoral.*)

A distinction should be drawn between *personal ethics* signifying the moral code applicable to individual persons, and *social ethics,* referring to moral theory concerned with groups. Inasmuch as moral theory is at the foundations of a good society or state, social ethics may be considered identical with social or political philosophy. Personal ethics, on the other hand, is restricted to the moral behavior of individuals. It should be noted that in this discussion ethics is interpreted broadly to include not only specific ideals or acts conforming to a formal code of morality, but also the entire pattern of moral ideals and behavior, the way of life, one's philosophy of life or *Weltanschauung.*

THE PHILOSOPHY OF SOCRATES

Socrates (470-399 B.C.) was one of the first of the ancient Greek thinkers to urge that scholars and leading citizens turn their attention from the study of external nature to the study of human nature, man himself. To Socrates man is the foremost consideration, and whatever affects man is of decisive importance, whereas knowledge of the world (cosmology), having no significant relationship to man, is of secondary value. All knowledge affecting mankind, which has a bearing on human life, is worth possessing, and, moreover, "the unexamined life is not worth living."

Know Thyself. To know oneself, that is to know oneself completely, one's conscious and unconscious self, makes for power, self-control, and success. Individuals encounter difficulty only because they do not truly know themselves—their natures, limitations, abilities, motives, the entire gamut of their personalities. They need a psychological mirror enabling each person to see his spiritual self as it really is, including all its shortcomings, strengths, and potentialities.

A man who truly knows himself will succeed, for he will know precisely what is within his capabilities, and the area in which to apply them, whereas the person who does not know himself will constantly blunder, even to the point of ruining his life.

Most people assume that they know themselves well, presumably because each is closer to himself than to anyone else, but proximity does not guarantee insight. In fact, a wise man can know you better than you are able to know yourself. Socrates asks, "Do you think you know yourself, merely because you know your own name?" He points out that if we want to know horses, we must ascertain their age, strength, and health in order to determine whether they are fast or slow, able or not able to work. The same principle applies to man; to know himself, a person must know all of the facts which have any relationship whatever to his existence. Self-knowledge is an essential good.

Virtue is Knowledge. For Socrates, anyone who knows the right thing to do will do it. Wrong actions are committed only out of ignorance. A person fails to do what is right because, and only because, he does not know what is right. No sane person will knowingly and willingly injure himself; if he does this, it will be through error, never intentionally. No one will deliberately choose to do what is wrong, for an evil deed is always harmful to the self as well as to others.

If people knew the real consequences of stealing, lying, cheating, hating, and other evils, how damaging these activities are to themselves, causing spiritual degradation and mental deterioration, they would certainly avoid them. The only reason people do not abstain from such deleterious behavior is that they do not realize the damaging consequences, for any man who knows what is right will automatically do it.

Virtue is Happiness. Not only is knowledge virtue, but virtue itself is identical with *happiness,* for a man who is doing what is right is doing that which is for his own good, resulting in happiness.

THE SELF-REALIZATION PHILOSOPHY OF ARISTOTLE

The system of ethical thought developed by Aristotle (384-322 B.C.) may be termed *Self-Realizationism,* based on the view that the good life or happiness is the result of fulfilling one's potentialities, character, or personality. The individual must convert his potentialities into actualities.

At birth the infant is not a person, but only potentially one; to be a real person, his potential must be "realized." Thus, an individual might be endowed with the musical sensitivity of a Beethoven, but if he were unaware of his talent or failed to cultivate it, he would remain merely a potential musician until he could develop his powers and function as a competent artist.

According to Aristotle, man's proper goal in life is to fulfill his potential, to realize his true nature or personality to the utmost and thus to attain perfection. An individual who fails to do this will suffer discontent as a consequence of his thwarted goals; his sense of frustration will show itself in the form of illness or unhappiness. On the other hand, the person who has realized his potential nature will experience happiness as a concomitant of fulfillment.

Nature Does Nothing in Vain.   Aristotle believes profoundly that "nature does nothing in vain"; whatever she does is done with a purpose. All things, living or dead, were created for a purpose; human beings have their own natural purposes, their proper functions and goals, the accomplishment of which brings beauty, a sense of satisfaction, and happiness. Compare man with a seed, which begins only as a potential flower, but grows into plant and blossom until it attains completion, beauty, fulfillment. So, too, man at birth is but a complex of potential characteristics, but he may develop his powers to become an artist, a musician, a scientist, a writer, an inventor, a beautiful being, a happy and complete man.

Life's Highest Good—Happiness.   Man, said Aristotle, pursues a great variety of goals, but the one he seeks as his ultimate end is *happiness*. All other purposes are only a means to achieve happiness, which alone is desired in and for itself. Money is a means, not an end. It is an instrument enabling the possessor to purchase things which will contribute to his personal happiness. Similarly, his daily work, marriage, civic activities, and property are a possible source of happiness. The pursuit of happiness gives meaning and purpose to man's life; indeed, if he were to be deprived of his chance to achieve happiness, his interest in living, his desire to continue, would cease.

The Path to Happiness.   According to Aristotle, the attainment of happiness depends entirely upon activation of each individual's powers and talents. This process of self-realization produces the happiest life; furthermore, the person who possesses the greatest innate potentiality enjoys the brightest prospect of happiness. Conversely, the individual whose potential remains unfulfilled will inevitably suffer extreme frustration and unhappiness. God created man for a purpose, and failure to realize that purpose brings discontent, whereas actualization of the self brings satisfaction, happiness, a beautiful state of mind.

The Highest Form of Happiness. As indicated above, Aristotle identified the *summum bonum,* life's greatest good, as happiness, which reaches a superlative form when man's highest nature is realized. Man's highest nature is to be found in the realm of the mind, in the mental aspects of life which are distinctively human; it is the fullest expression of thought (e.g., scientific or philosophical) that produces the greatest happiness. The human mind's highest ability is to think; hence *contemplation,* the activity of the mind, is the source of man's highest joy.

Man's Threefold Nature. Aristotle asserted that man has three natures, namely, the *vegetable* (physical), *animal* (emotional or sensual), and *rational* (human) nature. Each must be fulfilled; and the realization of each is accompanied by a state of happiness.

On the plane of vegetable nature, good physical health induces a sense of well-being, sustained by proper exercise and care of the body. Satisfaction of our animal nature brings more fulfillment, as in the enjoyment of appetites and instincts. It is on the third or rational level, however, that supreme happiness can be attained, and this happiness arises from the functions of human reason, fulfilling the potentialities of the mind. Consequently, a life of leisure is far superior to mere physical or animal experience; the life of reason is uniquely human, devoted to music, painting, art, beauty, philosophy, literature, science, politics, society, religion, humor, and all other intellectual interests which man enjoys but which are unknown to the lower species.

Moderation in All Things. Aristotle identified rational behavior with virtue. He defined virtue as habitual moderation, that is to say, the habitual avoidance of extreme modes of conduct. Extremes are always evil, while virtue is a mean between two extremes: for example, courage is a virtue between the two extremes of cowardice and recklessness. (At one extreme, the coward lacks courage; at the other extreme, the reckless person passes beyond the proper limits of courage, becomes a victim of his own ignorance and excessive boldness.) The virtuous person is one who practices virtuous conduct, not merely on one or two occasions but so frequently that he makes it habitual, and it becomes a trait of his personality. Conversely, immoral personality develops as a consequence of repeated acts of evil behavior.

Aristotelian Virtues.   There are numerous virtues, each representing a middle course between two extremes. Aristotle listed twelve important virtues and their associated vices, as follows:

VICE OF DEFICIENCY	VIRTUE OF MODERATION	VICE OF EXCESS
Cowardice	Courage	Foolhardiness
Insensibility	Temperance	Licentiousness
Illiberality	Liberality	Prodigality
Meanness	Magnificence	Vulgarity
Humility	Magnanimity	Vanity
Lack of Ambition	(Unnamed)	(Over) Ambitiousness
Impassivity	Gentleness	Irascibility
Self-Depreciation	Truthfulness	Boastfulness
Boorishness	Wittiness	Buffoonery
Quarrelsomeness	Friendliness	Obsequiousness or Flattery
Shamelessness	Modesty	Bashfulness
Maliciousness	Righteous Indignation	Envy
	Justice (the Sum of All Virtues)	

The Right Act.   Man, said Aristotle, should aim not merely to live but to live *well*, in accordance with the dictates of his reason, his highest nature. His conduct should be governed by the principle of virtue, requiring moderation and the avoidance of extremes. It is necessary to determine which course of action is virtuous, that is, the mean between extremes, and this is no easy task, for virtue means doing the right thing, in relation to the right person, at the right time, to the right extent, in the right manner, and for the right purpose. Thus, to give money away is quite a simple task, but for the act to be virtuous, the donor must give to the right person, for the right purpose, in the right amount, in the right manner, and at the right time—a very difficult obligation.

THE HEDONISTIC PHILOSOPHY OF EPICURUS

Hedonism is a system of philosophy which advocates the pursuit of pleasure and the avoidance of pain as primary objectives; man has only one moral obligation, namely, to gratify his desire for pleasure and to eradicate or at least minimize pain so far as possible. There are several schools of Hedonist thought, some of which emphasize momentary sensual pleasures, while others devote equal attention to spiritual pleasures as well. Some Hedonists, the Egoistic school, strive for the utmost self-gratification, irrespective of any painful consequences to others; but there is one Hedonist school, the Ideal Utilitarians, who approve only of those pleasures to which each individual is rightfully entitled and advocate as a goal the greatest possible benefits for all mankind.

Cyrenaic Hedonism. The Cyrenaic school, founded by Aristippus (435-356 B.C.), advocated immediate pleasures as the chief goal in life. "Eat, drink, and be merry, for tomorrow we die." It was their view that every momentary pleasure should be enjoyed to the full, lest the opportunity for such experience be lost forever. These Hedonists are not concerned with a possible future life but only with the pleasures of their present life, and they insist that, since pleasure is the only good, everyone should take advantage of all opportunities to enjoy such pleasures.

Epicureanism. Epicurus (342-270 B.C.) did not agree with the Cyrenaics in their indiscriminate acceptance of all pleasures, for he knew that many pleasures are detrimental and consequently should be avoided. Too often those who have tried to follow the philosophy of "eating, drinking, and making merry, for tomorrow we die" have encountered disaster because they did not die on the morrow, but lived to suffer the consequences of excessive or

ill-chosen pleasures. Accordingly, it behooves one to be discrim-
inating in selecting pleasures, for not all are of equal value, nor
are all equally desirable—that is to say, some pleasant experiences
should be rejected entirely, whereas certain painful experiences should be endured for the promise of a better future.
Epicurus would advise an ill person to take medicine or undergo
an operation for the sake of the greater good to follow.

The Summum Bonum—Prudence.   For Epicurus, prudence is
the greatest good; prudence is the best criterion of good and
desirable pleasures, for it can guide us to proper pleasures and
away from improper ones; and prudence may impel us to
undergo pain for the sake of a better future.

Indiscriminate and continual participation in pleasure may
dilute it, or cause it to disappear, or even convert it into pain.
Overindulgence in a particular food, for example, may soon make
one dislike it; here is an indication that *moderation* and contin-
ence are necessary if a person is to enjoy pleasures which will
retain their appeal.

Pain and Death.   Epicurus stressed the avoidance of pain much
more than the pursuit of pleasure, reasoning that life as such is
basically good, notwithstanding the incidence of pain, illness,
and fear of death. He considered fear, particularly fear of death,
a principal source of unhappiness and held that conquest over
the fear of death would make life pleasurable. To convince
people that they should give up their fear of death, he presented
them with logical arguments in the form of a dilemma: There
is no need to fear death because when we are alive, there is no
death to fear; and when we die, either we are nonexistent or
there is a life after death. If there is an immortality, then we
need not be concerned with death, and if there is no future life,
then we will not be able to fear or worry; accordingly, fear of
death is needless.

THE STOIC PHILOSOPHY OF EPICTETUS

According to the great Stoic philosopher Epictetus (A.D.
50-120) one of life's greatest values is contentment, a life of
tranquillity, serenity, and composure. There is nothing worth
becoming disturbed about; peace of mind is of superlative worth.

Peace of soul is gained through self-control or self-mastery, which is the ability to harness one's desires, commanding them instead of allowing them to rule.

To permit another person to disturb your mental equilibrium is to offer yourself in slavery to him, or even worse, because a slave is one in body only, whereas you have made your soul servile to him. Any person capable of angering you becomes your master; he can anger you only when you permit yourself to be disturbed by him. "If any person was intending to put your body in the power of any man whom you fell in with on the way, you would be vexed: but that you put your understanding in the power of any man whom you meet, so that if he should revile you, it is disturbed and troubled, are you not ashamed of this?" [1] We must not allow ourselves to become enslaved by anyone.

Objects which you desire intensely obtain a tenacious hold upon you; in order to become free it is necessary for you to extinguish your desire for all things, life itself as well as goods. If a man stole your most valuable watch, you would be upset because of your attachment for it, but if he were to steal an old worthless watch that you were about to discard anyway, then you would not be disturbed because it induced no desire on your part.

You can also preserve your serenity by understanding the true nature of things; thus, if you break an expensive piece of jewelry, then say to yourself, "After all, it is made of breakable material, hence it broke." If you realize that milk spills, then when it happens you are prepared for it, and your soul is braced against the damage. The same holds true for your attitude toward loved ones; if your child dies, said Epictetus, remind yourself that he is made of flesh and blood, mortal substance subject to destruction, and if your mind is steeled against life's emotional traumas, you will be able to endure them when they occur.

Stoic Resignation and Endurance. Stoic philosophy teaches us to accept what cannot be changed. We must learn to live with unavoidable disappointment, accept any loss whenever it occurs and tolerate it so that the sting will diminish and fade away. Most

---

[1] Quotations in this section are from *The Discourses of Epictetus,* tr. George Long.

of the misery of life comes from within, from our refusal to accept our portion in life. Thus, physical handicaps will become unendurable hardships if we allow them to overwhelm us, but if we accept such misfortunes as part of life, they grow less menacing and can be withstood. The great Stoic philosopher Epictetus learned this lesson from life experience, for he was both a slave, subjected to abuse and adversity, and physically handicapped.

The Unconquerable Will. Stoic philosophy emphasizes the doctrine that an individual's will must be kept inviolable and autonomous; it must be his own, never subjected to control by others. No one has power over a person's will unless he consents, which he should never do but rather should remain an independent and thus invincible spirit. Socrates is a superlative example of this doctrine, reflected in his statement, while awaiting death ordered by enemies who had planned to break his spirit: "Anytus and Meletus have power to put me to death, but not to harm me." In other words, these evil politicians, being unable to break the will of Socrates, were powerless over his spirit.

On harsh vicissitudes of life, Epictetus counseled:"What then should a man have in readiness in such circumstances? What else than this? What is mine and what is not mine; and what is permitted to me, and what is not permitted to me. I must die. Must I then die lamenting? I must be put in chains. Must I then also lament? I must go into exile. Does any man then hinder me from going with smiles and cheerfulness and contentment? . . . But I will put you in chains. Man, what are you talking about? Me, in chains? You may fetter my leg, but my will not even God himself can overpower. I will throw you into prison. My poor body, you mean. I will cut your head off. When then have I told you that my head alone cannot be cut off."

The secret of dying is to be "like a man who gives up what belongs to another"; furthermore, in losing anything to death, the attitude a person should assume is not that he has lost his life, but that "I have returned it." A person returns to God what God initially gave.

Problems of Life. Difficult problems of life, said Epictetus, should be embraced; one must never run away from them, for they are desirable spiritual exercises. Consider them as God wrestling with you, so that when the trial is over, you are a better man for it. As the body needs physical exercise in order to remain in fit condition, man's spirit also requires the spiritual exercise derived when he confronts his problems and combats life's vicissitudes.

The Stoic Philosophy of Sex. According to Epictetus, the cravings of sex are undesirable, for they merely enslave their victim. Abstinence is preferable to indulgence, which can be one of the strongest disturbances to the spirit's tranquillity. It is best to avoid all encounter with sex, inasmuch as no one can be caught in the clutches of a sex partner without disturbing consequences. "Today when I saw a handsome person," said Epictetus, "I did not say to myself, I wish I could lie with her, and happy is her husband; for he who says this says, happy is her adulterer also. Nor do I picture the rest to my mind: the woman present, and stripping herself and lying down by my side. I stroke my head and say, Well done, Epictetus. . . . And even if the woman is willing, and gives signs, and sends messages, and if she also fondle me and come close to me I should abstain and be victorious. Over such a victory as this a man may just justly be proud."

THE UTILITARIAN PHILOSOPHY OF JEREMY BENTHAM

The modern philosophy of Utilitarianism, which is actually very similar to Hedonism, owes its development largely to British philosophers, particularly Jeremy Bentham (1784-1832) and John Stuart Mill (1806-1873) who contributed significantly to the field of ethical theory. Utilitarianism, like Hedonism, defines the good in terms of pleasure but carries the principle further: it advocates as a basic aim the greatest good for the greatest number. Bentham explained this ideal as follows in his *An Introduction to the Principles of Morals and Legislation:* "By the principle of utility is meant that principle which approves or disapproves of every action whatsoever, according to the tendency which it appears to have to augment or diminish the happiness of the party whose interest is in question; or, what is the same

thing in other words, to promote or to oppose that happiness." [1]
He defined *utility* as any source of pleasure, happiness, benefit,
good, or advantage, or any means of prevention of pain, evil, and
unhappiness.

Quantitative Hedonism.   Bentham was a Quantitative Hedonist; that is, he believed that there is only one kind of pleasure,
that pleasures differ only quantitatively—e.g., in amount, duration, and intensity. Pleasures do not vary in quality, and there
is no real distinction basically between a sensual pleasure and a
spiritual pleasure. All pleasure is physical, sensual.

The Summum Bonum.   Bentham, who was a Materialist, repudiated spiritual pleasures, regarding them as pseudo-pleasures,
and asserted that physical pleasures are the greatest good attainable in life, and that, consequently, an individual deprived of
sensual pleasures will find life not worth living. Man's primary,
or perhaps sole, objective should be the pursuit of pleasure.

The Hedonistic Calculus.   Bentham feared that most people
might not always choose the best possible pleasures. For this
reason he contrived a device capable of measuring pleasure, a
Hedonist calculus, with seven points or criteria to facilitate a
correct choice between rival pleasures. Whenever the individual
found a situation in which he could not enjoy both of two
competing pleasures, he would resort to the Hedonistic calculus as a basis for his decision.

The seven points of the calculus are: (1) *intensity*—the degree,
strength, or force of the pleasure; (2) *duration*—the amount of
time the pleasure endures; (3) *certainty* or *uncertainty*—the degree of assurance that a specific experience will bring anticipated
pleasure; (4) *propinquity* or *remoteness*—closeness of the pleasure in space and time; (5) *fecundity*—the probability that one
pleasure may lead to additional subsequent pleasures; (6) *purity*
—the absence of painful elements; and (7) *extent*—the possibility
of sharing pleasures with others.

The Four Sanctions.   In order to guarantee that no person will
exceed the bounds of propriety in pursuing his particular pleas-

---

[1] Quotations in this section are from Jeremy Bentham, *An Introduction
to the Principles of Morals and Legislation* (London, 1780; rev. ed., 1823).

ures, Bentham cited four sanctions or deterrents which will prevent immoral excess: 1) the *physical sanction;* (2) the *political sanction*; (3) the *moral* or *popular sanction;* and (4) the *religious sanction.*

The four sanctions may be illustrated as follows: (1) If a person overeats, he will become satiated, nauseated, or ill—the physical sanction; (2) if a person steals his pleasures, he may be imprisoned—the political sanction; (3) if a person engages in unjust pleasures, he may be ostracized from society or he may be censured by public opinion—the moral or popular sanction; (4) if a person indulges in forbidden pleasures, immoral ones, then God will punish him either in this life or in the next—the religious sanction.

THE UTILITARIANISM OF JOHN STUART MILL

It was the initial intention of John Stuart Mill to defend and refine the Utilitarianism of Jeremy Bentham, but he eventually realized that his point of view had become incompatible with Benthamism. He had developed a critical attitude toward Bentham's basic premise that pleasure (sensual or physical pleasure) is the greatest good in life. If Bentham were correct, said Mill, and physical pleasure were the *summum bonum,* the highest possible good, then it would not matter whether the animal enjoying himself were a human being or a pig. Why, indeed, should the human being subject to pain and disappointment be considered superior to the perfectly satisfied pig if sensual pleasure were to be accepted as the greatest good?

Mill concluded that pleasures must differ from one another in quality. A small amount of human pleasure will therefore possess more value than a large amount of the kind of pleasure enjoyed by a pig. Mill's philosophy, contrasted with Bentham's Quantitative Hedonism, became known as Qualitative Hedonism.

The Criterion of Morality. It will be recalled that Bentham had devised a Hedonistic Calculus as his criterion of right action. Mill preferred a different criterion, namely, the opinion of a Hedonic expert, that is, a person who is in a position to decide the better of two pleasures because he has experienced both. If two people, both of whom have enjoyed each pleasure in question, disagree, then the verdict must be given by the more intelligent, because he is in the better position to render an accurate judgment.

Mill stated his view as follows:

If I am asked what I mean by difference of quality in pleasures, or what makes one pleasure more valuable than another, merely as a pleasure, except its being greater in amount, there is but one possible answer. Of two pleasures, if there be one to which all or almost all who have experience of both give a decided preference, irrespective of any feeling of moral obligation to prefer it, that is the more desirable pleasure. If one of the two is, by those who are competently acquainted with both, placed so far above the other that they prefer it, even though knowing it to be attended with a greater amount of discontent, and would not resign it for any quantity of the other pleasure which their nature is capable of, we are justified in ascribing to the preferred enjoyment a superiority in quality, so far outweighing quantity as to render it, in comparison, of small account.

"Now it is an unquestionable fact that those who are equally acquainted with, and equally capable of appreciating and enjoying both, do give a most marked preference to the manner of existence which employs their higher faculties. Few human creatures would consent to be changed into any of the lower animals, for a promise of the fullest allowance of a beast's pleasures; no intelligent human being would consent to be a fool, no instructed person would be an ignoramus, no person of feeling and conscience would be selfish and base, even though they should be persuaded that the fool, the dunce, or the rascal is better satisfied with his lot than they are with theirs . . . A being of higher faculties requires more to make him happy, is capable probably of more acute suffering, and is certainly accessible to it at more points, than one of an inferior type; but in spite of these liabilities, he can never really wish to sink into what he feels to be a lower grade of existence . . . It is better to be a human being dissatisfied than a pig satisfied; better to be Socrates dissatisfied than a fool satisfied. And if the fool, or the pig, is of a different opinion, it is because they only know their own side of the question. The other party to the comparison knows both sides." [1]

Everybody to Count for One, Nobody for More than One. Mill elaborated and incorporated into his own system Bentham's

---

[1] John Stuart Mill, *Utilitarianism* (London, 1863; 12th ed., 1895).

democratic dictum that happiness and the good of each person are as valuable to himself as the happiness and good of anyone else are to that person. Each person is therefore as important as any other, and must be so treated. The pauper becomes as important as the prince, and everyone in the world is placed on the same democratic footing of equality.

THE INTUITIONISM OF IMMANUEL KANT

The system of ethics formulated by Immanuel Kant (1724-1804) is based essentially on the concept of a good will, that is, a will with reverence for moral law; accordingly this system is technically termed *Deontological,* an ethics of duty. "Duty is the obligation to act from reverence for [moral] law." [1] The entire world of morality is contained in the realm of a rational good will. Kant stated in his Metaphysics of Morality: "Nothing in the whole world, or even outside of the world, can possibly be regarded as good without limitation except a *good will*." Where there is no will, no freedom of choice, a moral situation cannot possibly exist.

The Ethics of Intuitionism. The theory that morality is entirely within the individual, that moral values arise from his will and purposes (rather than from overt action dependent on consequences of an act) is termed *Intuitionism.* Kant held that only the will is good, irrespective of the results of overt actions. In fact, actions are morally neutral. The will, man's moral self, chooses according to the dictates of moral law. Right is right and must be willed regardless of consequences; "let justice be done though the heavens fall." When the moral law commands us to tell the truth or keep a promise, we must will to do so without regard for the possibly disastrous consequences to ourselves or to others.

The Categorical Imperative. Kant's criterion of morality (the means of testing whether an act is moral or immoral) is the Categorical Imperative: "Act as if the principle from which you act were to become through your will a universal law of nature."

---

[1] Quotations in this section are from Immanuel Kant, *The Metaphysics of Morality,* tr. John Watson (1901).

To decide whether a contemplated action is moral, one must apply this to it. Thus, the person who is about to break a solemn pledge must ask himself, "Can I will that everyone break promises, if he so chooses?" If the answer is negative, the proposed breach is immoral.

The Categorical Imperative is an unconditional moral command, holding true regardless of conditions; it matters not what the particular circumstances are, nor where and when they occur. The Imperative is unconditional (categorical), without restrictions or qualifications of any kind. If breaking promises is right in one instance or for one person, then it is right in all instances for all persons. What is wrong for one is wrong for all; thus we have in the Categorical Imperative a philosophical formulation of the Golden Rule: "Do unto others as you would have them do unto you."

Kant both illustrates and proves his point: "May I, for instance, under the pressure of circumstances, make a promise which I have no intention of keeping? The question is not, whether it is prudent to make a false promise, but whether it is morally right. To enable me to answer this question shortly and conclusively, the best way is for me to ask myself whether it would satisfy me that the principle to extricate myself from embarrassment by giving a false promise should have the force of a universal law, applying to others as well as to myself. And I see at once that, while I can certainly will the lie, I cannot will that lying should be a universal law. If lying were universal, there would, properly speaking, be no promises whatever. I might say that I intended to do a certain thing at some future time, but nobody would believe me, or if he did at the moment trust to my promise, he would afterwards pay me back in my own coin. My principle proves to be self-destructive, so soon as it is taken as a universal law." [1]

The Autonomy of Will.   According to Kant, morality is possible only because of the existence of a *rational good will* in human beings, a freedom of choice which is not coerced by anything but itself. The autonomous will adheres to its own dictates.

---

[1] *Ibid.* The term *maxim* has been replaced by *principle*.

No one can possibly force a person to will to do that which he does not choose to. Although a person may force a child to do an unpleasant act, he cannot make the child will to do it, unless the child so chooses for himself. The only way to make another individual's will coincide with one's own is to reason with him: if rational persuasion fails, no other way remains open.

The Dignity of Man. All objects except man, said Kant, have exchange value, a price for which they will be sold. Even an object with great sentimental value will be sold if an offer to buy is high enough, but man possesses dignity (infinite intrinsic value) and is therefore priceless. To the charge that "every man has his price," Kant would reply that any man who sold himself for money would be cheated out of his rightful due, for a man is above all price and possesses infinite worth.

Persons: A Kingdom of Ends. From Kant's point of view, it is because only human beings have an autonomous will (because they alone are moral agents, and moral values exist in and for persons solely) that they constitute a *kingdom of ends*; that is to say, we must treat people as an end in themselves, never as means only. Practically all persons can be put to some good use, and therefore have utilitarian value, but because they are also beings possessing *dignity*, infinite intrinsic value, should the time come when they have lost all utilitarian value (e.g., as completely helpless invalids), they must still be respected and aided as possessing infinite intrinsic worth.

Evil as Parasitic. Kant pointed out that evil lives a parasitic existence, that it is incapable of thriving on its own, but survives only on soil nurtured by goodness. A deceitful person could never deceive others were it not for the fact that most people under ordinary circumstances tell the truth. If the majority became habitual liars, no one could ever trust anyone else. Thus, even the temporary success of evil depends upon good; if the good were destroyed, evil would ultimately destroy itself, like a gang of bank robbers who work well together on the basis of loyalty to each other (a moral good) but eventually destroy themselves in a quarrel about sharing the loot.

The Universe as Basically Moral. Moral laws undergird the world, said Kant, so that a person who will strive (but vainly) to live an immoral existence will find that the moral laws by which the world is ordered will eventually frustrate his efforts. The attempt to carry on a society, an institution, or a business, on an immoral basis will never prove successful on any lasting basis. Thus the merchant whose sole concern is to make a profit regardless of the means used (fair or foul) will discover that cheating and deceiving his customers will in due time cost him patronage. Modern business proprietors value a good moral reputation as a substantial asset and expect any prospective purchaser of their business to pay for it under the heading of *good will*.

THE PESSIMISTIC PHILOSOPHY OF ARTHUR SCHOPENHAUER

The noted German philosopher Arthur Schopenhauer (1788-1860) believed that evil is positive rather than negative, that the world is basically and inherently evil. Happiness is experienced only during momentary respites between periods of unhappiness —and, in fact, happiness consists of this brief absence of pain, this temporary interval separating one evil experience from the next. As in popular fiction, the story must be ended when, after interminable vicissitudes, the hero and heroine are happily wedded, for if the narrative continued, the reality of repeated misfortune would eventually prove Schopenhauer's judgments that "life must be some kind of mistake," and that "it is a sin to be born."

Pessimism. Schopenhauer's philosophy of Pessimism is based on the contention that the world is an irrational blind force, without guidance, for there is no God to direct it. Reality, a blind force, is a potent *will,* which in man takes the form of insatiable instincts, drives, or desires. To satisfy a single desire leaves man laden with a number of unsatisfied others gnawing at him; desires abound, but satisfactions are relatively few. In real life most people experience either frustration or, in the event of occasional success, complete boredom.

In Schopenhauer's words: "All *willing* arises from want, therefore from deficiency, and therefore from suffering. The satisfaction of a wish ends it; yet for one wish that is satisfied there remain at least ten which are denied. Further, the desire lasts long, the demands are infinite; the satisfaction is short and scantily measured out. But even the final satisfaction is itself only apparent; every satisfied wish at once makes room for a new one; both are illusions. . . . No attained object of desire can give lasting satisfaction, but merely a fleeting gratification; it is like alms thrown to the beggar, that keeps him alive today that his misery may be prolonged till the morrow." [1]

Suicide provides no escape. In the first place, it is a final irreversible act motivated by considerations which might turn out to be a gross blunder. In the second place, the will, i.e., the tormenting forces of this world, is eternal, and consequently will persist in the afterlife.

Escape from Evil (Human Salvation).   For Schopenhauer, there is one means of escape from the misery of this world—extinction of desires. Repudiate the desire for life, but not for life itself. Annihilate the will, desires and instincts, and be content with nothingness, a state of Nirvana (absence of desire). One might think that contemplation of Platonic Ideals (which, being independent of space and time, are free from the sting of will and instincts) could also bring relief, but this mode of escape can at best achieve only partial salvation.

An Ethics of Sympathy.   Schopenhauer recognizes the necessity for compassion. Inasmuch as every person's life is tragic, and each experiences his special torment, he must not condemn another for evil actions, but pity him. We are all "in the same boat" caught where we do not wish to be, without much control over our wretched state; therefore it is unwise to condemn a neighbor, and we should show him compassion to help alleviate his condition. "It is this compassion alone which is the real basis of all *voluntary* justice and all *genuine loving-kindness*. Only so far as an action springs therefrom, has it moral value; and all conduct that proceeds from any other motive whatever has none. When once compassion is stirred within me by another's pain, then his weal and woe go straight to my heart, exactly in the same way, if not always to the same degree, as otherwise I feel only my

[1] Arthur Schopenhauer, *The World as Will and Idea,* tr. R. B. Haldane and J. Kemp (1883).

own. Consequently the difference between myself and him is no longer an absolute one." [1]

THE NATURALISTIC PHILOSOPHY OF FRIEDRICH NIETZSCHE

Friedrich Nietzsche (1844-1900) believed that contemporary morality is an inversion of true morality. Whatever is genuinely moral accords with human nature and never contradicts it. Nietzsche agreed with Schopenhauer that man's nature is composed of life instincts, that the task of life is to fulfill man's instincts, not to inhibit them as the prevailing culture of modern times has so often demanded. But he differed profoundly from Schopenhauer's pessimism, assuring us, on the contrary, that success is attainable if we give full expression to our instincts instead of repressing them.

Slave Morality vs. Master Morality.   Nietsche pointed out that two moral systems have been apparent throughout history—that of enslaved peoples and that of the elite who have traditionally ruled—and that each system has had its own moral code. The slave morality of the weak requires them to accept subjugation and obedience to the master race.

The *master morality* consists of the ethics of the aristocratic class (rulers and noblemen) who comprise the "Aryan race' of conquerors," dedicated to combat, adventure, victory. For these men, peace comes only with conquest of their opponents who must then acknowledge the natural right of the strong to rule the weak.

The principle that *might makes right,* said Nietzsche, is the verdict of nature, in contrast to civilization (Christian and Jewish) which has opposed this ethic with one of humility and compassion. The traditional Judeo-Christian culture is appropriate, Nietzsche insisted, only for slaves. The Jews were a subject people during most of their history and consequently developed a morality suited to the weaker segment of the human race. Theirs

---

[1] Arthur Schopenhauer, *The Basis of Morality,* tr. Arthur Brodick Bullock (1903).

is an ethic of *ressentiment,* a product of repressed anger, a repressed hostility which seeks to devise hidden reprisals against their lords and taskmasters. According to Nietzsche, slaves do not dare to retaliate openly but seek clandestine forms of revenge.

Nietzsche accused Judeo-Christian religious leaders of using religion as a means of turning natural moral values upside down, so that the master race became the slaves, and the slaves became the masters. The slaves, said he, became priests representing the omnipotent God and threatened their masters with divine punishment unless they, the masters, accepted a humble, servile role as obedient servants of the slaves. Nietzsche called for a revaluation of all values, the repudiation of Judeo-Christian values. (Note the kinship of this philosophy to that of Adolph Hitler, although Nietzsche's aristocrats were to be found in many nations, not in one only.)

The Superman. Nietsche's Superman is a moral giant endowed with physical superiority. He is a member of a race to come; no one has yet achieved this high goal, for the best of men have fallen short. The Nietzschean concept of Superman would require him to be a being who combined the might and majesty of Caesar with the moral superiority of Jesus.

Just as man is superior to the ape, so the Superman will be distinctly superior to man. As a morally superior creation, Superman never needs to grant forgiveness, for he would promptly forget or ignore any wrongs done him. In fact, he has forgiven even before he has been wronged. In spirit he is like Jesus on the cross, asking God to forgive his enemies. Nietzsche asserted that Jesus was an ideal model for Christians, but they had failed to imitate that model and, consequently, "there was only one Christian and he died on the cross." [1]

Thus Spake Zarathustra. Although Nietzsche was an atheist, he was a most perceptive critic of those who profess to believe in God, yet deny him by their reprehensible behavior. Nietzsche depicts a mythical Persian oracle, Zarathustra, as jeering at an

---

[1] Friedrich Nietzsche, *The Antichrist,* tr. Walter Kaufman (New York: The Viking Press, Inc., 1954).

old saint in the forest: "Could it be possible! This old saint in the forest hath not yet heard of it, that *God is dead*." [1] In other words, if we judge from the behavior of Jews and Christians, God must be dead; if he were not, then those who believe in him would not dare to misbehave so abominably.

The fact that God died for love of man, said Nietzsche, proves that love brings suffering and misfortune. Love makes the individual vulnerable to evil influences and adverse circumstances. Thus the illness of a loved one may affect him more than his own. The individual must not be dissuaded from self-realization by consideration of sentimental attachments of this kind, but must always remember that God died for love of man because of man's incorrigible behavior.

ROYCE'S PHILOSOPHY OF LOYALTY

The great American philosopher Josiah Royce (1855-1916) defined his philosophy of loyalty as *"the willing and practical and thoroughgoing devotion* of a person to a cause." [2] Loyalty is the supreme good in life, and within it is contained all other virtues. There are times when one's loyalties conflict, but, when this occurs, it is necessary to be "loyal to loyalty."

Loyalty—The Supreme Good. Loyalty is the *summum bonum,* the greatest good man can experience; further, it is always good regardless of the cause which enlists a person's loyalty. Although a cause may be bad, loyalty is never bad, even if devoted to an ill-advised cause. Consequently, it would be unquestionably wrong to destroy the spirit of loyalty, though it be within an individual who has allied himself to a detrimental cause.

If one's loyalty is attached to an unworthy object, one should seek to associate its fine spirit with a cause more worthy of a person's devotion. Thus it is the *spirit* of loyalty which is good; the cause to which it is put is a matter for an enlightened intelligence to decide.

Loyalty to Loyalty. When loyalties conflict, a person should

---

[1] Friedrich Nietzsche, *Thus Spake Zarathustra,* tr. Thomas Common (New York: The Macmillan Co., 1930).

[2] Josiah Royce, *The Philosophy of Loyalty* (New York: The Macmillan Co., 1908).

nevertheless be loyal to loyalty. He should be true to the spirit of loyalty, not to destroy loyalty wherever it is found, not to diminish it, but to enhance it. If he discovers that other people are loyal to an evil cause, he must never attempt to lessen or destroy their endeavor, but only to enlist their support for a worthier cause. It is necessary to preserve intact the beautiful spirit of loyalty within each individual; to do otherwise, to injure his spirit of loyalty, would be an action of disloyalty to the spirit of loyalty.

THE ETHICAL REALISM OF GEORGE EDWARD MOORE

George Edward Moore (1873-1958) expounded Ideal Utilitarianism as a philosophy antithetical to Intuitionism; the Intuitionist asserts that all morality resides within the individual as a matter of will, intention, or predisposition. The Ideal Utilitarian describes the moral realm in terms of overt action, consequences, and external events, whereas Moore defines actions as right or wrong on the basis of the effects caused regardless of the doer's intent. The principle states that "the question whether an action is right or wrong always depends upon its total consequences." [1] If the total consequences make the world a better place in which to live, the act is moral; if not, the act must be wrong.

The right act is not merely the best intended one, nor is it even the best foreseeable under existing conditions, but that act which produces the *best possible actual consequences*. It is not the predictable consequences which are tallied in the final accounting of right and wrong, but the actual results.

The major difficulty with the ethics of Ideal Utilitarianism is the inability of a person ever to know whether his actions will actually turn out to be the best possible; only an omniscient mind could know that, and hence only God's actions could satisfy the requirements of this ethic.

Moore's doctrine of Ethical Realism states that genuine ethical properties exist in the overt moral act itself, independent of the human mind's ascribing any moral value to it. Morality is ex-

---

[1] George Edward Moore, *Ethics* (London: Oxford University Press, 1912), p. 106.

ternal to human consciousness; an act may be truly good or bad whether or not a person participates in it or is even aware of it. This view is directly contrary to that of Intuitionism, which restricts morality to the individual's conscious purpose and experience without regard to consequences.

Moore considered a good act a *Gestalt,* an organic whole which cannot be severed into parts. The whole is greater than the sum of its parts. Water is wet, yet there is no wetness in either hydrogen or oxygen, elements out of which water is composed. Just as water has properties which are not found in an analysis of its component parts, ethical acts have moral properties which cannot be discovered through analysis. It is true, for example, that a man who has rescued a child from drowning obviously has performed a good deed, but analyzing the situation into the various aspects of which his entire act is composed will never account for his *goodness* per se. Does the goodness of his act consist of his getting wet? Of his successful effort to grasp the child? Of his movements in pulling the youngster to shore? No one of these elements involved in the entire act can be said to constitute its *goodness,* yet the entirety, as a whole, is recognized as good. Goodness is real, but it is an organic unity, a value found in the whole, not detectable in its parts considered individually.

The Indefinability of Good.   Moore contended that good is indefinable because it is an ultimate, simplest term. To define a word, it is necessary to break it down into simpler elements of which it is comprised, but what happens when it becomes necessary to define the simplest terms used to define others? The simplest word *good* is ultimate and, although it may be used to define other things, is itself indefinable.

The Naturalistic Fallacy.   According to Moore, goodness is an experience; either you do experience goodness, or you are incapable of it. Just as a blind person cannot experience the color yellow, and as far as he (the blind person) is concerned, yellow does not exist for him, so the same kind of incapacity holds true for beings unable to experience goodness. Although it is possible to point out good things (food, clothing, shelter, etc.), it is impossible to define goodness itself. Those who think that they have been successful in defining goodness because they have been able to offer a scientific explanation of good things, have committed what Moore terms the *Naturalistic Fallacy*. We would commit the same fallacy if we tried to give a blind person a scientific explanation of the color yellow and concluded that we had in this way enabled him to experience the yellow color itself.

PART THREE—SOCIAL, POLITICAL, AND LEGAL PHILOSOPHY

PART THREE—SOCIAL, POLITICAL, AND LEGAL PHILOSOPHY

The development of social, political, and legal philosophy in the Western philosophical tradition can be traced back as early as Plato (427-347 B.C.); and ever since the Platonic period, philosophers have sought to determine the nature and meaning of the good society, the good State, and just laws; that is to say, what a society and a State ought to be. Their interpretations have been formulated as diverse concepts of an ideal State, a *utopia* (the Greek term meaning *no place*). Today, as in the past, these utopian thinkers exert considerable influence on political affairs, especially in America and in Communist countries, where individuals trained in this field of philosophy attain a prominent role in government service. (In the United States comparable dependence has been placed on the study of law.)

PLATO'S REPUBLIC

Plato was faced with a problem which he strove to resolve, namely, *injustice;* eventually, he resolved the matter, the solution to which was *justice.* The following discussion summarizes some of his basic ideas about the cause, nature, and resolution of injustice, and the definition, nature, and institutions of justice.

Relationship between the State and Individuals. Plato's political philosophy rests upon his principles that the individual is more important than society and that it is necessary to know the nature of individuals in order to ascertain the characteristics of a desirable society. The good society depends upon virtuous persons, and virtue depends upon the character of individual citizens. It is not necessarily the system of society itself which creates evil social conditions, but it is the individuals who populate it. Good people produce a good State, while corrupt people engender corrupt politics.

59

The Four Cardinal Virtues.   In Plato's view, moral values and conduct depend upon the psychological traits of man, which in turn depend upon biological characteristics. Plato identified the three major biological aspects of man with the head, the heart, and the stomach, each with its own natural function—the rational, the spiritual, and the appetitive, respectively—and each with its own natural virtue.

Plato defined virtue as *excellence,* which can be achieved in any of the three phases of human life, corresponding to the rational, the spiritual, and the appetitive function. The person who excels in the art of reasoning possesses the virtue of *wisdom;* he who excels in the application of energy (determination) possesses the virtue of *courage*; and he who excels in the control of his appetites (self-control) possesses the virtue of *moderation*. All people share in the three types of natural functions, but only those who excel in them can be said to possess these virtues.

The Nature and Role of Justice.   For Plato justice is a concomitant virtue; that is, it is a result of harmonious co-operation among virtuous individuals participating in affairs of the State. Justice prevails only when each person assumes his responsible part in the State and contributes to it according to his virtuous talents. In a just society each man does what he is best fitted to do by nature, accepting the task which he is most able to accomplish; not only does he perform his own special work, but he minds his own business as well. Indeed, said Plato, interference with others who are attempting to carry on their proper tasks creates conflict and disharmony, the essence of injustice. A chaotic situation of injustice results when each person vainly attempts to do what he has no talent, training, or ability to do; justice prevails and a good State exists when each person performs tasks for which he is qualified by natural talent (virtue) and training.

The Organization of the Good State.   In the good State, political organization and personnel depend upon the virtues of each member. Plato's ideal State has three major classes: (1) The teaching class, or *guardians,* entrusted with the responsibilities of government and instruction; this class is composed of individuals possessing the virtue, wisdom. (2) The *warrior* class, consisting of courageous persons who excel in spirit and will power; they fulfill the duty of protecting the State from its enemies, domestic or foreign. (3) The working class, or *artisans,* who possess the virtue of moderation (self-control) and assume the task customarily performed by the masses of laborers, farmers, tradesmen, and merchants; these men carry out instructions well, for they have learned obedience, a virtue which enables them to hold their desires in check.

Education in the Good State. It is necessary, said Plato, to select and train individual members of the State on the basis of their respective talents so that they will be able to cultivate their corresponding virtues. This undertaking can be accomplished through democratic education. At an early age children will be enrolled in school and will be given equal opportunity to demonstrate their native abilities. When the children reach adolescence, those best fitted to become artisans will be chosen and assigned to jobs appropriate to their talents. A few years later, in a second process of selection, the warrior class will graduate from school and enter upon their duties. Only the guardians will remain in school to obtain intensive instruction in dialectics and philosophy, and also to serve as apprentices in responsible positions. The fully trained guardians will be expected to become leaders of the State in view of their moral character, training in philosophy, and superior intellect.

A Political Aristocracy. The foregoing discussion has indicated a stratification of society; although each person would enjoy equal opportunity to seek the highest·positions in the State, and the educational opportunities would be established on a democratic basis, only the best would be allowed to fill positions of high responsibility, as in teaching and public service.

Any public official who far excelled the others would become *monarch,* but if no one comparable to Socrates in wisdom were available, then a group of the best qualified persons would rule as a senate, an *aristocracy.* These aristocrats in the senate would live as Communists, holding no property of their own during the period of public service, in order to minimize or eliminate corruption. The purpose would be to prevent nepotism and bribery.

Plato regarded an aristocracy as the form of government generally best (monarchy would be a perfect choice if the peerless leader were available) and he analyzed four imperfect forms: (1) timocracy, or government by men of honor and excellence —one in which the national heroes and warriors are entrusted with political control. Timocracy may degenerate into (2) oligarchy, or the rule of a few motivated by selfish monetary gain; since the common people in such a State respect wealth and hold the rich in high esteem, the latter easily obtain control and achieve their evil purposes. Oligarchy may then give way to (3) democracy, or government by the people on the basis of equality; since a pure democracy lacks a constitution which could check emotionally volatile masses, it tends to be erratic, driven by its whims and fancies, and is really an inefficient form of government run by the poor and untrained. Democracy may then give way to (4) tyranny, a one-man dictatorship, the worst of the four.

To Plato, then, the most wholesome government is a *Republic,* administered by an aristocracy of the best qualified persons (morally and intellectually) although he would prefer a monarch even to a republic if there were to be found that superior person—the philosopher-king—who could rule with perfect wisdom and justice. "Until kings become philosophers, or philosophers kings, there is no hope for the State."

THE POLITICAL PHILOSOPHY OF ARISTOTLE

Aristotle (384-322 B.C.), like Plato before him, based the theory of the good State on the nature of man, but, whereas Plato gave the individual priority over the State, Aristotle reversed this relationship. He said that man is by nature a political and social animal, that the individual cannot live a wholesome, normal, or good life without society. A hermit leads an abnormal existence which distorts his natural character. Living in solitude is contrary to the nature and interest of man. In truth, said Aristotle, the goal of every human being is to fulfill himself, his nature, in order to grow to full maturity and enjoy happiness, and this highest good (happiness) is attainable only in a society.

Thus we see that society was not made for man, for his convenience and disposition, but is a vital necessity, an indispensable need which man cannot do without. This being the case, individual ethics must be subordinated to social ethics (politics), and the individual must willingly sacrifice himself for the State. The truth is not that society needs man but that, conversely, man needs society, for society is a moral idea arising out of the needs of mankind.

Aim of the State. If man is to develop wholesomely, fulfill his needs (biological, social, intellectual, cultural), he must do so within the social matrix. Furthermore, since the State is a moral idea, its aim is ethical, and it builds character, it is a necessity if man is to achieve his moral goals. The basic objective of the State is to prepare persons for a life of leisure in which man's highest good can be realized—a life which can be devoted to cultural pursuits, religion, art, political activity, scientific research, or, best of all, philosophy.

In the Aristotelian world, citizenship was to be only for the upper classes; slaves and peasants, being poor, would be compelled to work; and inasmuch as only the upper classes could devote themselves to leisure activities of politics, science, and philosophy, they alone would have an opportunity to achieve the good life, *happiness,* the by-product of moral excellence.

The Good State. For Aristotle, good government is a relative matter; there is no best form for all peoples at all times. A good government is one whose rulers seek the welfare of the people, whereas a corrupt government is one whose rulers are primarily interested in selfish ends. A good government may therefore degenerate into a corrupt one if the rulers begin to devote themselves to private gain instead of public welfare. Thus each good form of government has its corresponding corrupt form, as follows:

GOOD FORMS	CORRUPT FORMS
Monarchy	Tyranny
Aristocracy	Oligarchy
Polity (Constitutional Government)	Democracy

As indicated above, in a *Monarchy* one particularly outstanding leader rules, and he is interested in the nation's welfare, not in private gain. It is only when the monarch ceases to be concerned about the good of his people, and seeks to accumulate wealth and power for selfish purposes, that the government degenerates into a Tyranny.

Similarly, in an *Aristocracy,* which should be governed by the best citizens, it sometimes happens that the rulers slight the public welfare and seek mainly their private ends so that the government deteriorates into an Oligarchy misruled by a rich minority.

Finally, in a *Polity* there is constitutional government run by a considerable number of qualified people, and this form degenerates into a Democracy only if the multitude of ruling personnel ignore the good of the State and its citizens and exploit power for their own advantage. In democracy, the corrupt form, the masses decide policy for the sake of personal gain rather than the good of the State.

Political Moderation.   Aristotle applied the principle of "moderation in all things" to the problem of evaluating any State: for example, was it too large or too small for its population and location, or for the character and skills of its people? He concluded that the good State is one in which the middle class constitutes a majority, for a nation with an excess of lower class poverty-stricken individuals will tax the State unduly, becoming a serious handicap, a welfare State, while an excess of the upper classes interested in personal wealth will also create national imbalance. A middle-class majority together with middle-class rule is the healthiest condition for a nation.

Extremes should always be avoided, for too many individuals in a given occupation will disturb the equilibrium of the State. Too many soldiers, too many public officials, or too many of any other group except the great middle class will injure or even destroy the State. Aristotle cited the example of Sparta which was destroyed by overemphasis on the military way of life: "The Spartans ever geared for war and not for peace, in times of peace rusted as a sword in a scabbard." Since the basic nature of man requires peace, not war, the State must be organized for peace so that it may survive and prosper.

THE LEGAL PHILOSOPHY OF SAINT THOMAS AQUINAS

According to Saint Thomas Aquinas (A.D. 1225-1274), God is the supreme lawgiver, creator of all laws, divine or natural, from which in turn human laws are derived. Saint Thomas held that the social order and its just laws follow the pattern which God has imbedded throughout nature. Unjust laws, however, inasmuch as they could not have emanated from God, cannot be regarded as genuine laws. Although, strictly speaking, it is not man's duty to obey unjust laws, there is a moral justification for requiring obedience to men in power, for "all power is from the Lord God." Man must be subject to the powers that be, since "there is no power except from God."

To have dominion is to possess power, that is, to be above or higher than something or someone. To resist power is to resist God's ordinance, i.e., a command which God has decided "to order." It is a kind of *ordination,* classified into three orders: (1) Dominions, (2) Powers, and (3) Principalities. Although these three orders refer to a celestial hierarchy (angelic orders), they apply equally to the ecclesiastical hierarchy (church orders) and to the political hierarchy (social order). In secular society, the Chief of State functions according to the order of God, with all subordinates and subjects required to obey his commands; he has been ordained by God. Saint Thomas maintained that even an unjust act of an evil ruler becomes indirectly an *act of God.*

Violence and Civil Disobedience. Saint Thomas further held that a proper and just relationship between civil power and public order makes violence unnecessary and establishes peace. Violence is repugnant except as a last resort, and even then the violence used in resisting evil must not be greater than is required for this purpose. Since violence is contrary to nature, it can very seldom fulfill the intended will of God. For this reason an individual compelled to choose between resistance and submission to violence will usually find it best to submit, but he should certainly know what is at stake and protest against the evil.

There is a difference, said Saint Thomas, between laws which are unjust in relation to God, and laws which are merely unfair in relation to ourselves. We must never conform to laws in the first category. But in regard to the second category of unjust

laws—those detrimental to human beings—our reaction is a matter of individual conscience and we may accordingly choose to
denounce or to obey, or perhaps even to submit to violence. An
innocent man condemned to death is justified in attempting to
escape, but a guilty person does not have the same right. As a
practical matter it may sometimes be desirable that the innocent
suffer unjust punishment in order to avoid scandal; such was the
case with Socrates, who went to his death as a means of dramatiz-
ing justice; he chose to respect the sanctity of law and appeal to
reason instead of directly resisting evil deeds.

Natural Law.   Logical reasoning, in Saint Thomas' view, is the
proper basis for evaluation of human conduct, but natural law
determines the pattern of logical reasoning. It should be noted
that natural law involves not merely the actual functions of the
human organism, but especially a moral quality which makes it
the *moral law* as well. Man may freely choose either to obey and
pursue the natural law or to pervert it. All aberration of the
natural law is immoral.

Saint Thomas believed that knowledge of the natural law is
not acquired through reasoning as such but through *connaturality,* an inclination enabling us to comprehend any good
which accords with our nature. Through reason we can appreciate
that this inclination is good and that the distortion of natural
law is bad. But the unwritten laws of nature become known to
us by means of our natural reaction to the world, through connaturality, without requiring the aid of rational (conceptual)
knowledge.

These inclinations which make human knowledge possible are
not mere animal instincts, but consist of nonconceptual precon-
scious ontological life in harmony with reason. Furthermore, they
are rooted in reason in the sense that they operate as rational
moral dictates, self-evident principles, mandates, which command
us to do good and shun evil. The specific natural laws we discover
are founded upon the inclinations of our own human nature.
In earliest times man's natural inclinations were uniformly
authentic paths to moral understanding, but later some of them
were at times adulterated or mixed with perverted, counterfeit
ideas or tendencies.

Eternal Law. In Thomistic philosophy the meaning of eternal law, although such law emanates from God, must be derived by philosophical means rather than by divine theology. The eternal God who exists, the initial activator of all other beings, acts by his will and intellect; hence the government of the universe is directed according to divine reason—which is to say, *natural law is the reason of God in action*. The reason of God, his eternal wisdom, his divine essence, becomes one with eternal law, this being the expression of divine wisdom which directs both action and movement of things.

Natural law is related to eternal law through participation in it, and from divine reason it obtains its rational character, its obligatory or moral character, and its genuine nature as law. The obligatory power of natural law is contingent upon the existence of God—*no God, then no morality*. The unwritten eternal law is validated by the divine intellect, and is apprehended in itself by God alone or by those capable of seeing God in his essence.

Positive Law. In Thomistic philosophy, positive law, that is to say, *written law*, is identical with positive right, for the concept of right (juridical order) is imposed on the individual and enforced by society, and thus becomes a legal debt the neglect of which renders a person liable to punishment. While the dictates of positive right (positive law) are sanctions of society (legal sanctions) natural law is a moral sanction with priority over positive law. Natural law, which is unwritten, obligates our conscience concerning the moral, not the juridical, order; hence natural law involves a moral debt rather than a legal one.

Natural Right. The right of self-defense is an example of natural right, which comes into play as an accompaniment of natural law. Natural right is expressed verbally as a precept setting forth a positive right in a juridical order. It is implicit in natural law.

National and International Law. The *jus gentium* or law of nations is the common law of civilization, but it differs from natural law in that it is not known through inclination, but only through reason and intellectual concepts. The law of nations, even though it may not have been codified verbally, is nevertheless a juridical order obtained by the conceptual exercise of human reason. Thus, the prescription that the laws of society should be obeyed is a rational rule which the intellect accepts as valid wherever man is to live in a group. The law of nations is implicated both in the moral and in the juridical order, for it commands from us both a moral and a legal obligation.

MACHIAVELLI'S POLITICAL PHILOSOPHY

Niccolo Machiavelli (1469-1527) propounded the doctrine that justified any ruler in using every means necessary, fair or foul, to maintain a strong government. The end justifies the means, even though that end be for the sole benefit of the tyrant.

To gain political power, it is necessary either to be the child of fortune and be born into power, or to acquire power through deceit and conquest. Since power will be attained by treachery with the assistance of cobelligerents (who themselves are evil enough to participate in the malicious techniques), it will become necessary to eliminate them. Moreover, in destroying enemies within the State, the ruler must get rid of them decisively without mercy, lest some individual suffering from minor injuries return to seek revenge.

A Prince's regard for his subjects should be limited to the extent necessary to maintain full personal power. The ruler may appear devoted to ideals of mercy, faith, integrity, humanity, and religion in order to create an excellent public image, but often he must act contrary to those ideas; consequently he needs above all to develop a hypocritical, vascillating personality. Only a few perceptive individuals will discover his real character and they will not dare protest or move against the vulgar tide adhering to the mighty Prince. Thus the ruler will continue to hold the balance of power.

The Prince. Machiavelli's classic work, *The Prince*, analyzes the problem of to what extent and by what means Princes should keep faith with their subjects. His answer is that Princes should keep faith with their people by resorting to both law and force; since law often proves ineffectual, force is called for, even though force has ordinarily been used to control beasts.

In brief, the Prince should display a dual character—thirsting for power like a lion while using deceit and cunning like a fox. He should be cautious, bearing in mind that a lion cannot defend himself from traps, nor can a fox from wolves. The two qualities complement each other. Like a fox, the Prince can disguise his true character, appearing to be virtuous, even though he may be cruel and often needs to be merciless. Any Prince foolish enough to be truly virtuous will forfeit his kingdom to enemies; to retain his power, it is imperative for him to pose as a virtuous ruler.

The Forms of Government. Machiavelli held that throughout history there have been only two basic forms of government, namely, *Princedoms* (Monarchies) and *Republics* (Free States), of which Republics are the superior form. Republics cannot be successfully inaugurated without virtuous citizens, however, and since the masses are corrupt, only Princedoms are feasible. Furthermore, the fact that the corrupt masses need to be controlled justifies deceitful and vicious behavior, for *"the end justifies the means."*

THE POLITICAL PHILOSOPHY OF THOMAS HOBBES

The political philosophy of Thomas Hobbes (1588-1679) is based upon a Social Contract theory which contributed theoretical foundations for modern democracies. A distinction must be made, however, between Hobbes' belief in the inalienable rights of man as natural rights and the modern concept of human rights as those rights granted by a divine Being.

Hobbes declared that man is fundamentally an untrustworthy, corrupt being who has to protect himself from his fellows just as beasts in the jungle do. Each person finds it necessary to lock his doors against burglars and even to lock his chest against thieving members of his own household. Man is not only so corrupt but also so quarrelsome and belligerent that, except for very brief intervals between quarrels, he is constantly fighting others. There are three main reasons for human aggressiveness, namely, competition (for self-gain), distrust of others (based on the need for self-preservation), and thirst for glory (the need to be looked up to or respected). Competition impels men toward violence, distrust of others calls for a strategy of self-defense, and the thirst for glory requires subtle diplomatic tactics.

Natural Rights.   In Hobbes' view, nature's law governing the behavior of all creatures is the law of the jungle, the "law of tooth and claw." In accord with this law that might makes right, the jungle lion seizes what justly belongs to him, while others in turn take what they can, and man must do the same, even if he finds it necessary to enslave and kill. "Every man has a right to everything; even to one another's body." [1]

Human Equality.   As indicated above, nature's law allows any person to do whatever he pleases within the limits of his physical powers, for in the animal kingdom "nothing can be unjust." Man must be more cunning than beasts, however, lest his fellows repel his attacks or retaliate. Even the weakest person equipped with sufficiently superior weapons and tactics can subdue the strongest of men. Hobbes pointed out that groups of men tend to be more or less equal in power and that for this reason a relatively weak individual can join a group for self-defense against a physically superior enemy. "For as to the strength of the body, the weakest has strength enough to kill the strongest, either by secret machination, or by confederacy with others, that are in the same danger with himself." Hobbes agreed with the old adage, "United we stand, divided we fall."

Natural Law.   Hobbes believed that, in accordance with nature's basic law, the individual must protect his own life at any cost or sacrifice, for there is no cause worth the risk of death. Self-preservation is the first law of nature, which impels man to "seek peace and follow it." The fear of injury or death and the instinct for self-preservation keep man from destroying himself and others. This first natural law (the law of self-preservation) has compelled human beings to comply with a second law, that of the social contract, for self-preservation is best attained in a society in which there is lasting peace based on such a contract.

The Social Contract.   For Hobbes, the social contract is essen-

---

[1] Quotations in this section are from Thomas Hobbes, *Leviathan* (London, 1651).

tially a means of establishing civil rights by implementing the Golden Rule ("Do unto others that which you would have them do to you") instead of nature's law that might makes right. The individual gains civil rights by entering into a compact with his fellows which is based on the principle "that a man be willing for the sake of peace, to lay down his natural right, and be content to limit his liberties to the extent that others are willing to curb theirs." This principle constitutes a second law the importance of which is exceeded only by that of the first basic law of nature—the law of self-preservation.

Laws Emanating from the Social Contract. From the above it is clear that the second law developed out of the first, for man entered into the social contract in order to insure his self-preservation. Hobbes pointed out that a number of other laws are implied by the first two. He summarized the various laws as follows:

1. "Man is forbidden to do that which is destructive of his life" (the law of self-preservation).
2. "That a man be willing, when others so too, as far forth, as for peace, and defence of himself he shall think it necessary to lay down this right to all things; and be contented with so much liberty against other men as he would allow other men against himself" (the law of the Social Contract).
3. "That men perform their covenants made" (the law of justice).
4. "That a man which receiveth benefit from another of mere grace, endeavour that he which giveth it, have. no reasonable cause to repent him of his good will" (the law of gratitude).
5. "That every man strive to accommodate himself to the rest" (the law of compliance).
6. After warning, "a man ought to pardon the past offenses of them that repenting, desire it" (the law of pardon).
7. In matters of revenge, (retribution of evil for evil), men should not look "at the greatness of the evil past, but the greatness of the good to follow" (the law of revenge).
8. "That no man by deed, word, countenance, or gesture, declare hatred, or contempt of another" (the law of contempt).
9. "Every man acknowledge another for his equal by nature" (the law of pride).

10. On entering into "conditions of peace, no man require to reserve to himself any right, which he is not content should be reserved to every one of the rest" (the law of arrogance and modesty).

11. Those things which cannot be divided, "be enjoyed in common, if it can be; and if the quantity of the thing permit, without stint; otherwise proportionably to the number of them that have right" (the law of equity).

12. The entire right be determined by lot, or first possession (corollary of the law of equity).

13. "All men that mediate peace, be allowed safe conduct" (the law of safe conduct).

14. "They that are at controversy, submit their right to the judgment of an arbitrator" (the law of arbitration).

Note that these laws, according to Hobbes, are elaborations upon or inferences from the Golden Rule.

The Leviathan.   The laws incumbent upon the individual citizen entering into the social contract are indeed highly commendable, but a crucial question is raised: What happens if one party to the contract refuses or fails to live up to the responsibilities by which he is bound? Hobbes answers that a power greater than those who are party to the contract, though he himself (the power) does not participate in the contract and is not bound by it, does see that those who have so engaged do fulfill their obligations under penalty of punishment. The individual who is thus empowered to act, and who is himself above the law (immune), is called the *Leviathan,* a mortal god, whose power to so act issues from natural right, for he is the strongest power on earth (or at least in the nation). This power is assumed to be the king, but if a power mightier than he should arise on the horizon and subdue him, then the new potentate would become the Leviathan.

Where there is no king, with absolute power, the contract is made with an assembly of men, and the State is called a *Commonwealth* (a Political Commonwealth or a Commonwealth by Institution); but when it is established by the sovereign power, the king (either by natural force or by agreement of the engaging parties), it is termed a Commonwealth by Acquisition.

THE DEMOCRATIC PHILOSOPHY OF
JEAN JACQUES ROUSSEAU

The democratic philosophy of Jean Jacques Rousseau (1712-1778) emphasized the principle that sovereignty resides in the people, that all other power is dependent upon this fundamental sovereign power. States are established on the basis of a *social contract* entered into for the sake of the security and well-being of their citizens; hence sovereignty exists for the protection of individuals, and in obeying the laws the individuals are merely submitting themselves to their own mandates. The government possesses delegated power, not absolute or sovereign power, for an inalienable right issues from the will of the people as a corporate body; it is the will of this body politic, a general will, which government officials must execute. The general will is for the benefit of all. Moreover, the State must not be so large or cumbersome as to prevent citizens from becoming acquainted with one another; and the best form of government is one administered by a small group of elected officials.

Freedom and Equality. Modern civilization is an aberration of nature, for "man is born free and everywhere he is in chains." [1] Society, a perversion of nature, has abrogated the inalienable rights of man. The earliest societies were arranged on the order of the family, the nearest and truest form of natural society; accordingly, the family should be taken as the paradigm for contemporary political societies. In a family each child is born free and equal by birth, and the same principle should prevail in political affairs of States as well.

The idea of slavery is repugnant in a free society, for "might does not make right," nor does a man have "natural authority over his fellow men." It therefore follows that since societies cannot legitimately be organized by force, they are founded on conventions, a social contract.

The Inalienable Right of Sovereignty. Absolute sovereignty rests with the citizens as a body politic, for they alone are in

---

[1] Quotations in this section are from Jean Jacques Rousseau, *The Social Contract*, tr. Henry J. Tozer (London: Swan Sonnenschein and Co. Ltd.; 3rd ed., 1902).

possession of an inalienable will. Each individual *will* shares in the *general will* which ought to prevail for the good of all. Although power may be delegated, *will* cannot be delegated. "Sovereignty being nothing but the exercise of the general will, can never be alienated." For the same reason that sovereignty is inalienable, it is indivisible.

The General Will. The general will is not the simple enumeration of individual wills, yet it is expressed in the political activity of each citizen, unhampered by pressure, as he honestly and sincerely registers his independent conviction in a vote. A tally of votes may merely disclose individuals casting their lots for selfish desires, but the general will of the people reflects the sincere and honest expression of each person voting for that which will be good for the entire citizenry. "There is often a great deal of difference between the will of all and the general will; the latter regards only the common interest, while the former has regard to private interests, and is merely a sum of particular wills. . . . The general will is always right." A well-informed people, avoiding cliques and party factions, will give expression to the general will.

The Social Contract. Rousseau maintained that, since society is based on a social contract which provides for the defense and protection of its citizens and their property by utilizing the whole force of the community, each person, having joined with the rest, is independently free, obeying no one but himself. When a member of society breaks the laws, he has breached his own code. He will be punished not only to restore the equilibrium of society, but also to advance his own benefit because the social contract exists for the sake of each person's welfare.

The social contract is based on the fundamental principle that sovereignty belongs to the people (who possess inalienable wills). Power is transferable, but *will* never. Consequently, the government is merely the agent of the populace, operating under its directive, executing the general will. It can never wield absolute or final authority.

As to the form of an ideal State, Rousseau favored a Republic ruled by laws, in which the government, run by popularly elected officials, would implement the general will. He believed that the particular political structure is of minor consequence, but offered a rule of thumb for deciding this matter; small States should be a Democracy; middle-sized States, an Aristocracy; and large States, a Monarchy. He concluded that "if there existed a people of gods, it would govern itself democratically."

HEGEL'S PHILOSOPHY OF LAW

The political and legal philosophy of Georg Wilhelm Friedrich Hegel (1770-1831) is delineated in his *Die Philosophie des Rechts* (*The Philosophy of Law*). The German *Recht* may have any of three meanings of the English term "right": *moral principle; law;* or *civil right.* In fact, Hegel and many other German philosophers used the term to convey all three meanings.

The State: A Divine and Moral Idea. Like Aristotle, Hegel considered man a social being who can find his identity or reality only in the State. Man's reality is unrealizable unless identified with society; thus the State is essential to the realization of a moral idea. The State is an all-inclusive entity, a synthesis of man and all his institutions (including religion), the latter being necessarily subordinate to the State as a whole. Above all, the State must not be interpreted in terms of a social contract, as it is not created by the decisions of individuals.

No truth, or for that matter no full self-realization, either of an individual person or of institutions, can be attained except through the State, the sole condition by which a particular end or good can be achieved. The State is a real entity, not a mere assemblage of individuals. It is only in the State that individuals can progress from partial to complete self-realization.

Hegel identified the State with the power of God progressing throughout world history; it is an Idea, or God manifesting himself on earth, consequently worthy of being worshipped. As a perfect expression of rationality, the State requires of individuals only that which is rational. Although the State coheres through force, a basic sense of order holds it together.

The State An Organism. To Hegel the State is an organic whole in constant process of development, the unfolding of which is self-consciousness. A sick State is comparable to a sick human body which may exist, yet cannot function as a real entity; it is comparable, for example, to a severed hand which still appears to be a hand, but is devoid of significant reality as such. The State pursues a self-conscious course, which the World-Spirit has created for itself.

The Constitution. The State is the nation's spirit, the law permeating its entire life, including its ethical code and the consciousness of its citizens. The type of constitution a State adopts will be commensurate with the level of its self-consciousness, of its self-understanding, or of its progress toward perfect self-realization. A constitution is not created by men out of whole cloth but issues out of the level of awareness, of self-conscious attainment, developed throughout the historical life of the State. The constitution is rational and perpetual, hence divine, not a human instrument, but the work of centuries of history; it is the unfolding of the idea of what is rational, and the consciousness of what is rational. It is the sacred character of reason, a great "architectonic edifice."

The Monarch. Hegel designated Constitutional Monarchy the highest form of State, not democratic in the sense that sovereignty resides in the people, but representative in the sense that the ruler is the figurehead of an organic totality, exemplifying the World Spirit; he asserted that "sovereignty is in the personality of the whole, and this is represented in the person of the monarch." Final decisions rest with the State as a self-determining and completely sovereign will, and the monarch speaks for the totalitarian organ, the State. The person of the monarch is not the State *per se*, though the State acts through him so that in practice he has merely to "sign his name" to identify the spirit of the State. Since the State endures and is independent of the particular reigning monarch, however, his character (moral or immoral) is of little consequence. His qualifications are of minor import because he is a temporary "yes man" for the State and is required merely to "dot the *i*"; that is to say, despite the fact that immediate decisions rest with him, he merely provides the final touches and administers the decisions in accord with the State's sovereign will.

The monarch is the dictator ruling in a totalitarian State in which the executives and legislature merely act in an advisory capacity. Within the legislature, the interests of the masses (their views and desires) are permitted expression. Despite the fact that the masses are practically devoid of any power, the government should not display a hostile attitude toward them.

The masses find their unity, their organization, and their real identity in the State. The individual has no significance apart from the State.

Hegel's Philosophy of War. Hegel declared that war has an ethical aspect which ennobles human activity, that it summons forth the highest in man, giving him the opportunity to behave heroically, even to the extent of sacrificing his life for the State. Although the individual dies, the State lives on, and the State is greater than any individual. Personal valor is far less important than "self-subordination to a universal cause," to the service of the State. War tests the health and strength of nations and helps to preserve their moral vigor. Immanuel Kant was mistaken in his advocacy of perpetual peace, which actually produces decay, corruption, and deterioration, whereas war acts as a deterrent against such evils. In perpetual peace, organs become inactive and death ensues. In fact, said Hegel, without conflict there can be no progress, and war is conflict in its most accelerated and emphatic form. Thus from war, the greatest progress issues; nations emerge from their war invigorated. Without war, there can be no peace, for peace is the outcome of war.

International Relations. The State is the ultimate or final organ of the people. Consequently, since one State is not above another, one cannot dictate to another. Grievances between individuals are resolved by the State, but quarrels among nations are decided by war, and as to the question as to which nation is in the right, the verdict of history remains, "world history is world judgment," which is comparable to saying whatever happens to be the case, is right, a theory which can justify "might makes right."

In the same sense that individuals are not true persons unless related to the State, the State is not fully real unless related to other States. The whole comprises the course of history, the World-Spirit on the march in the world. The dialectic which rages among individual States eventuates in an unlimited World Spirit, one pronouncing judgment upon individual finite States and upon world history, "for the history of the world is the world's court of justice."

THE COMMUNISM OF KARL MARX

The foremost philosopher of Communism was Karl Marx (1818-1883) from whom proceeds the line of the great three: Marx-Engels-Lenin. The most popular of his (nonacademic) writings is *The Manifesto of the Communist Party* (1848), written in collaboration with Friedrich Engels (1820-1895), while his scholarly masterpiece is *Capital* (1867). Lenin's greatest philosophical work is *Materialism and Empirico-Criticism* (1909). The following major tenets of Communism are largely but not exclusively Marx's. (Engels gave Marx the principal credit for them.)

Communism: Defined. Contrary to a widespread assumption, Communism is essentially a philosophy advocating the "common ownership of the means of production," or, from another point of view, the "abolition of private property." No individual person (or limited group of persons) may monopolize property, except for minor personal belongings, because property belongs to the people as a whole. Whenever property can be privately owned, "exploitation of the many by the few" results.

The Labor Theory of Value. Consumer goods as such lack inherent monetary value: their price is a concomitant of the man hours of labor expended in the manufacture of the product. The greater number of man hours spent in production, the higher the selling price. "We see then that which determines the magnitude of the value of any article is the amount of labor socially necessary, or the labour-time socially necessary for its production. . . . The value of a commodity would therefore remain constant if the labour-time required for its production also remained constant." [1] However, an article which is useless, irrespective of the man hours cost to produce it, is worth nothing, for without some utilitarian value, an object is valueless.

---

[1] Karl Marx, *Capital* (1867).

The Classless Society. According to Engels, the most important doctrine of Marx is that of *Inherent Class War* raging between two irreconcilable groups: capitalist employers (the Bourgeoisie) and the workers (the Proletariat). Since the interests of each class are diametrically opposed and in conflict with each other, the only solution is to eliminate one, the Bourgeoisie, for they fail to contribute any work to society, and hence are social parasites. In the Communistic society, all must contribute: "From each according to his abilities, to each according to his needs!" [1]

The Bourgeoisie are responsible for a number of social evils: They have exploited the employee by giving him less than he has rightly earned; they have treated the worker as a commodity on the market, whose wage is dependent upon the fluctuations of the labor market, not upon the worth of the work produced. They have commercialized most occupations, including the professions, and most social institutions, such as marriage.

With the elimination of the capitalistic class, society will be at peace for, with but a single class, it will be a classless society composed of those who contribute either mental or manual work.

Dictatorship of the Proletariat. The single remaining class, the Proletariat (worker), will assume all responsibility not only for labor and management, but also for the administration of government. Only the Proletariat has a right to rule by virtue of its contribution to the State; hence the government must be a "Dictatorship of the Proletariat." They, the class of Proletariat, shall rule over themselves, but the time will come when the State will no longer be necessary in a world made up solely of workers; in that day we will experience a "withering away of the State." (This latter doctrine of the withering away of the State has baffled many Marxian experts.)

The Theory of Violent Revolution. Inasmuch as the ruling class will not voluntarily relinquish their wealth, capital, and power, it becomes necessary to abrogate them by force, i.e., by violence if necessary. Since their wealth and power rightfully belong to the working class, the Proletariat is justified in taking

---

[1] Karl Marx, *Critique of the Gotha Program* (1875).

it by force. "The Communists . . . openly declare that their ends can be attained only by the forcible overthrow of all existing social conditions. Let the ruling classes tremble at a Communistic revolution. . . . Working men of all countries, unite." Such are the concluding words of the *Manifesto of the Communist Party*.

Dialectical Materialism.   All goods are material, and material goods are the sources of power. He who controls capital controls also the culture of the people—their morals, religion, education, public opinion, music, art, etc.; those who control mass media (newspapers, radio, television) can manipulate public opinion and politics; those who control music publishing houses and recording companies can manipulate the musical tastes of the nation.

Since material goods, capital, are the sources of power, it is necessary to centralize "all instruments of production in the hands of the State." The cherished beliefs of any generation are essentially those imposed upon them by the class holding power. "What else does the history of ideas prove than that intellectual production changes in character in proportion as material production is changed? The ruling ideas of each age have ever been the ideas of its ruling class." [1]

Economic Determinism.   Economic determinism, the theory that the course of history is determined by economic factors, will eventually lead all nations to a Communistic Socialism. Whether nations work toward this end or not, is not of major consequence, for it is inevitable that Communism will ultimately emerge from all existing societies, as each society carries the "germs of its own destruction." The Communist answer to those who unsuccessfully attempt a revolution is, "the proper time is not yet mature."

Communist Measures of Social Reform.   The *Manifesto of the Communist Party* lists ten measures of social reform, as follows:

1. Abolition of property in land and application of all rents of land to public purposes.
2. A heavy progressive or graduated income tax.
3. Abolition of all right of inheritance.
4. Confiscation of the property of all emigrants and rebels.

---

[1] Karl Marx and Friedrich Engels, *Manifesto of the Communist Party* (1848).

5. Centralization of credit in the hands of the State by means of a national bank with State capital and an exclusive monopoly.

6. Centralization of the means of communication and transport in the hands of the State.

7. Extension of State ownership of factories and instruments of production; the bringing into cultivation of waste lands, and the improvement of the soil generally in accordance with a common plan.

8. Equal liability of all to labor. Establishment of industrial armies, especially for agriculture.

9. Combination of agriculture with manufacturing industries; gradual abolition of the distinction between town and country by a more equable distribution of the population over the country.

10. Free education for all children in public schools. Abolition of child labor in its present form. Combination of education with industrial production.

PART FOUR—PHILOSOPHY OF RELIGION

PART FOUR—PHILOSOPHY OF RELIGION

The philosopher's task is the *critical evaluation of all the facts of experience;* accordingly the philosophy of religion treats the critical evaluation of all the facts of religious experience, principally: God, soul, immortality, and natural evil.

The key term in the above definition is *evaluation,* for there are sciences of religion (psychology of religion, sociology of religion, and history of religion) which do not evaluate. The sciences of religion, as sciences, *describe* facts of religious experience as accurately and objectively as possible without evaluating religious beliefs as to their validity. It remains for philosophers of religion to evaluate religious experience and ascertain whether religious values are true or untrue. For example, the sociologist, studying the religions of India with meticulous care and accuracy, may assert that Hindus are Pantheists, believing in God as the totality of nature, but the philosopher of religion does not rest content with the mere fact that Hindus believe in Pantheism. He inquires whether Pantheism is a true or false belief, consistent or inconsistent, good or bad, moral or immoral; that is to say, he evaluates rather than restricts himself to mere description.

Philosophy of religion should not be confused with religion, nor with theology; religion involves acting upon one's philosophical convictions regarding religious experience, whereas philosophy limits itself to an evaluation of religious beliefs. Theology (revealed theology, dogmatic theology, or sacred theology) is distinct from the philosophy of religion. The philosopher's quest is unrestricted by bias, authority, revelation, or faith, seizing upon all pertinent data as a means of attaining the most coherent evaluation. Consequently, the facts of science, of nature, and the conclusions of reason are taken into consideration and given a careful accounting, whereas theology is content to accept on faith the validity of revelation, the inspiration of Holy Scripture, and the teachings of the Church. Claiming privileges of divine inspiration as a source of truth, theology enters areas which the philosopher considers unverifiable (such as Christology, soteriology, eschatology) and from which dogmatic doctrines emerge (such as the doctrine of the Trinity, which the philosopher avoids owing to its nonempirical and nonrational nature, rendering it incapable of rational scrutiny and validation).

Natural theology (philosophical theology), however, is identical with the philosophy of religion and should not be confused with revealed or dogmatic theology. Like the philosophy of religion, theology must be differentiated from religion *per se,* for theology is theoretical, whereas religious persons actually practice their faith, as in prayer; the theologian becomes religious only when he is committed to and practices the beliefs to which he adheres. A similar parallel may be drawn between philosophy and religion.

CONCEPTIONS OF GOD

Some philosophers of religion consider concepts regarding Deity as of paramount importance, taking precedence over all other concepts in the philosophy of religion. The primary question is no longer the existence of God but the significance of the term *God,* inasmuch as any definition of God implies existence. The meaning of the term may vary widely with the individual. To some, *God* denotes a Supreme Being, to others, nature or a universal principle.

Philosophers who assume that everyone has some concept of the Deity or a Supreme Being ask the question, How should *God* be defined? In one definition, every person might be considered religious, at least in the sense that the object he prizes most (or depends upon, or is committed to) is his God. Such a definition implies that the alcoholic's God might be the liquor upon which he depends for security; that the God of others might be the sciences in which they put their unshakable faith; that the God of some individuals might be the power (based perhaps on weapons such as the atomic bomb) which they seek for the sake of self-defense or security; and that the God of many others might be that Supreme Creator, or Personal Deity, in whom they repose their faith and confidence.

The following concepts of God have been dominant in the philosophy of religion.

Polytheism. In Polytheism, the belief in a plurality of gods, a god is defined as any one among a group of deities, each representing a unique personal value. Polytheists cherish each god as a being who assumes stewardship over and personifies a given value which men prize; thus there are the gods of fertility, of love, and so on. The Polytheist who feels the dire need of health prays to the spirit who is believed to control and therefore to have the power to bestow the desired state of good health upon the individual.

The modern scientist, who believes in a single system of laws, in one universe, in a unified power, ridicules Polytheism, for he cannot accept the notion of diverse, discordant supreme beings or multiple all-powerful deities. In science there is no separate system of natural laws for biology, another for physics, still another for chemistry, etc., but only one system valid for all branches of science. Actually, the scientist believes, not in many varieties of science, but in one unified science valid for one world, a *universe*. Consequently, from this point of view, the power (one God) lying behind the universe must be *unified*. On the other hand, Polytheism envisions many worlds (a "polyverse" rather than a universe), each with its own god at cross purposes with the others. Scientific order, as we know it today, can find no basis for such a view.

Henotheism. Coined by Max Müller, the term *Henotheism* refers to the belief in one God, yet not excluding all other gods. Henotheists depict God as *personified national spirit,* a national God, rather than as an international or universal God. Thus, in a given nation where more than one God is countenanced, one is elevated to a rank superior to the rest; such was the role of Zeus among the Greeks, and that of Jahwe among the Israelites. Although Moses declared the oneness of God, and the Hebrews regarded him as supreme, they granted a certain status to gods of other nations.

Pantheism. The Pantheists believe in the *to pan* (the all) of classical Greek philosophers, i.e., the idea that only God exists and that all that exists is God. Pantheism assumes various forms. The most common form emphasizes the totality of reality, but the doctrine may refer to the universe taken as a whole or to the combined forces (laws) of the universe. The religion of Pantheism is widely accepted among the Hindus of India, whereas in the Western world, it has been espoused mainly by a few individuals, including the philosophers Spinoza, Hegel, and Royce.

Other philosophers have pointed out that two basic deficiencies are inherent in Pantheism: the allocation of error to God's mind; and the attribution of evil to God's nature.

The first deficiency involves self-contradiction. Since every person is part of God, it follows that if a child (also part of God) believes erroneously that $2 + 2 = 5$, while at the same time his teacher (part of God as well) knows that $2 + 2 = 4$ and that the child is mistaken, the entire situation is one in which God must be assumed to be simultaneously aware and not aware that he is in error. Thus, Pantheism injects contradiction in the mind of God, an inconceivable impossibility.

The second deficiency, as set forth in the writings of Borden Parker Bowne, stems from the Pantheistic view that portrays God as the most evil of all beings; inasmuch as God is the sum total of all persons, he is more wicked than any single individual. The argument that God is also the sum total of all good persons does not acquit him of the responsibility for evils committed.

Monotheism. The various religions of Monotheism, based on the central belief that there exists one and only one God, view God as the *supreme personal creator,* the exclusive and universal creator of all things. In the history of civilization, this idea of one God has evolved from Polytheism, or more accurately Henotheism, to Monotheism. The monotheistic idea has been ascribed to Moses, although some contemporary religious schools consider Moses a Henotheist and date the monotheistic principle much later than the Mosaic period.

As indicated above, monotheistic creeds envision God as a self-existent personal spirit, the creator of all the universe and the source of all value. The major philosophical problem of Monotheism is how to explain the fact that, if God created *all* things, he must be the source or creator of both good and evil.

Theism. The doctrine of Theism differs from that of Monotheism proper in its emphasis upon the *personal* nature of God, conceiving him as *a conscious mind immanent in physical nature, man, and values of which he is either the source or the creator*. The God of the present Western world, of Judeo-Christian culture, is Theistic, a God possessing the personal attributes of goodness, intelligence, will, etc., which enable man to communicate with him in prayer, communion, and meditation.

Theists understand God as both transcendent (independent of and distinct from the world he created) and immanent (presently active in his creation, in the world of nature and moral values). Pantheists identify God with nature (eliminating transcendence completely); for them nature includes God, whereas Theists regard God's being as distinct from and independent of nature, even though (unlike the Deists) they adhere to the belief that God is also an active participant in all events of creation, including those of man as well as nature.

Deism. The Deists, while accepting the belief of Monotheism in one God, and the emphasis of Theism upon a personal God as the creator of the universe, view God as outside of the world which he has created. For the Deist, God is completely transcendent, lacking immanence in the world, and hence is the antithesis of the Pantheist deity. According to Deists, God, having created the universe so that it functions thereafter as a machine governed by its laws (of nature), divorced himself from the world and merely contemplates it from beyond as a disinterested bystander, or "absentee" deity, who neither heeds prayer nor chooses to perform miracles. God did all that he planned, rendered the world capable of self-perpetuation on the basis of natural law, gave man intelligence to understand and control nature and to detect in nature the creative activity of the divine power. In these activities man finds happiness, without interference by God, who "helps those who help themselves."

Deism as a systematic philosophy originated with Lord Herbert of Cherbury (1583-1648) and became a popular doctrine among American and British intellectuals. Among American adherents were Thomas Paine, Thomas Jefferson, and other Colonial statesmen; among the extremely influential British proponents were John Toland (*Christianity, Not Mysterious,* 1695) and Matthew Tindal (*Christianity as Old as the Creation,* 1730). In the contemporary world, however, the physical and biological sciences portray the universe, not as a machine, but as a dynamic, organic, growing process which cannot be explained adequately by reference only to the laws of mechanics. The dynamic nature of the world is emphasized particularly in modern theories of organic evolution.

Deistic Supernaturalism.   Another philosophy of religion, Deistic Supernaturalism, views God as transcendent, external to the world which he created, yet as the *superhuman and supernatural revealer of values.* Originating with Søren Kierkegaard (1813-1855), father of Existentialism and Neo-Orthodoxy, this belief is shared by many contemporary Protestant Fundamentalists. Deistic Supernaturalists deny that the nature of God can be detected in man's experience, while affirming that it issues from revelation by God himself.

Like the Deist, the Supernatural Deist understands God to be transcendent, beyond the world he created. The world, created some time ago, runs by itself. Unlike the Deist, however, the Supernatural Deist believes that communion with God can be established through prayer, and that God may answer prayer by disrupting the laws of nature in order to perform a miracle. (As we shall see, the Humanists reject this idea that God is wholly transcendent, known through nonhuman sources; the same idea is also diametrically opposed to Religious Naturalism.)

Humanism.   Antithetical to Supernaturalism, Humanism regards God as man's highest aspirations, reflecting man's pursuit of ideal values and embodying the sum of humanity. Comte, father of Humanism and of Classical Positivism, depicted God as Humanity, the Grand Being (*le Grande Être*) as he called him. Another leading Humanist, Ludwig Feuerbach, reduced God's objective existence to a subjective one residing in man's mind, a mere psychological entity, a product of man's idealized consciousness. In *The Essence of Christianity*, he wrote: "Man has his highest being, his God, in himself. . . . The Feeling of God is nothing else than man's highest feeling ·of self; . . . God is man, man is God."

Religious Humanism. Closely related to Humanism, the contemporary philosophy of religion known as Religious Humanism portrays God as man's highest social experience. The ideals of men prompt them to action, to become God. Noted humanists adhering to this view include John Dewey, Max C. Otto, and Roy Wood Sellars.

Impersonal Idealism. The philosophy of Impersonal Idealism equates ideals with God. Edward Gleason Spaulding, Impersonal Idealism's most articulate spokesman, wrote: "God is the totality of values, both existent and subsistent and of those agencies and efficiencies with which these values are identical." [1] Thus God, as understood here, is impersonal, a system of ideal values worthy of worship—eternal Platonic ideals of justice, beauty, truth, and goodness. These ideals are worshipped, in contrast to Theism which worships God as the source of them.

Agnostic Realism. The belief that God is the unknowable source of all which exists is known as Agnostic Realism. Its chief adherent, Herbert Spencer, wrote in his *First Principles* (1862): "By continually seeking to know and being continually thrown back with a deepened conviction of the impossibility of knowing, we may keep alive the consciousness that it is alike our highest wisdom and our highest duty to regard that through which all things exist as *The Unknowable*."

Panentheism. The concept of God as immanently interpenetrating all nature, yet distinct from it, is the central principle of Panentheism. God possesses self-identity and is independent of the particular objects of nature, though immanent in them. Panentheism differs from Deism .which posits only a transcendent God; it also differs from Pantheism which identifies God with nature. That is to say, it agrees with Pantheism that the being of God includes nature, but adds the belief that God surpasses

---

[1] Edward Gleason Spaulding, *The New Rationalism* (New York: Henry Holt and Co., 1918), p. 517.

and embraces more than nature. Among leading Panentheists are Edgar Sheffield Brightman, Albert Schweitzer, and Alfred North Whitehead.

Religious Naturalism.   In Religious Naturalism, a variant form of Materialism, God is portrayed as an ongoing, natural process or principle which creates and conserves moral values. Religious Naturalism, unlike traditional philosophies of Materialism, asserts that nature is a living, creative, developmental process, not a mechanistic conglomeration of inert atoms and that, furthermore, the creative activity of nature is unpredictable as to the new emergent properties to be produced. Unlike Monotheists who regard God as creator of nature, Religious Naturalists consider nature an eternal cosmic process. Outstanding proponents of this view include Samuel Alexander and Henry Nelson Wieman; the latter defined God as "the growth of meaning and value in the world."

In addition to the foregoing philosophies of religion, there are a number of relatively minor ones, such as Animism and Pansychism, which attract very few adherents and present an unsystematic or obscure conception of God and nature. Thus, Animism attributes life as we know it to stones and other physical objects, while Pansychism endows all natural objects with both physical and mental characteristics.

THE PROBLEM OF GOD'S EXISTENCE

Perhaps the most complex problem confronting the philosopher of religion is the question regarding God's existence, for the premise of a good God opens the way to a belief in the immortality of the soul; the strongest arguments for eternal life are predicated on the existence of a beneficent God. Earlier, it was noted that the conflict between Theism and Atheism is not the primary issue, and that the basic problem has to do with the nature of God; to a considerable extent, that is true, yet usually when people debate concerning God's existence they refer to a Theistic God. Consequently, the following discussion will deal with the arguments for a personal Creator, including the Deity as the source (*axiogenesis*) and preserver (*axiosoteria*) of value.

The Etiological Argument.   The idea that the world requires a First Cause which is itself uncaused is the basis of the Etiological

Argument for God. In its simplest form, this argument states that, since nothing contingent (man or nature) can ultimately be its own cause, then some noncontingent (necessary) Being must exist for this world to have come into existence—that because it would have been impossible for the universe to get started on its own initiative, an initial cause (God) was necessary.

Skeptical philosophers have accepted Hume's objection to the Etiological Argument, namely, the assertion that the world always existed; philosophers defending the argument, however, ask why it is that, if Hume's view be granted, man nevertheless persists in thinking of phenomenal nature (the physical world) as contingent, coming into being at a given point in time? Thus William Paley (1743-1805) argued (in opposition to Hume) that if finite nature is contingent and hence requires a cause, certainly an infinite nature would still require a cause; if a chain of a few links could not be suspended in mid-air without support, similarly a chain with an infinite number of links could not remain suspended in the same way.

The Cosmological Argument. As noted above, the Etiological Argument posits the existence of God on the ground that the world requires a First Cause; consequently that argument may be regarded as one aspect of the Cosmological Argument which bases the proof of God's existence on the fact of an orderly universe. From Cosmology, the study of order in the universe, this argument draws evidence for the conclusion that God was the source of world order. The logic of the Cosmological Argument rests on the thesis that the natural world is incapable of explaining itself; since an orderly universe is an effect, it is necessary to assume that a First Cause produced it.

Although the Etiological Argument is actually but one aspect of the Cosmological Argument, many philosophers use the two interchangeably, and further conclude that order in nature implies purpose. In this way they pass from the Etiological and Cosmological Arguments to consideration of a related concept, that of teleology.

The Teleological Argument. The existence of purpose in the world and the conclusion that such purpose is evidence of a Supreme Mind are basic assumptions of the Teleological Argument. During the Age of Reason, philosophers found purpose, design, and order in the universe, accepting the view that purpose is implicit in world design and order; with widespread approval of the Darwinian Theory of Evolution, however, philosophers during the past century have cited the evolutionary progress of the world as an organism and the adaptation of organisms to their environment as evidence of purpose in nature.

Argument from Design.   Paley became the most influential defender of the idea that God's existence is proved by the design to be found throughout nature. Paley's classic Watch Argument states that someone finding a watch on the ground would never conclude that the watch had been lying there forever, but rather (noting that the watch parts had been carefully designed to operate in harmonious conjunction with other parts for the purpose of telling time) would assume that an intelligent being had planned, devised, and constructed it. "There cannot be design without a designer; contrivance without a contriver; order without choice; arrangement without anything capable of arranging; subserviency and relation to a purpose without that which could intend a purpose; means suitable to an end, and executing their office in accomplishing that end, without ever having been contemplated or the means accommodated to it. Arrangement, disposition of parts, subserviency of means to an end, relation of instruments to a use imply the presence of intelligence and mind." [1]

Argument from Adaptation.   Paley's argument was challenged by adherents of Darwin's Theory of Evolution which purports to explain the designed order of the world by reference to the doctrine of the survival of the fittest. According to Darwin, natural design results when characteristics favorable to survival persist while the useless characteristics disappear. Paley's idea that world order indicates a beneficent Creator failed to explain evil, waste, pain, and disease—all those phenomena (apparently purposeless) known to philosophers as dysteleological; Darwin had explained them as part of the evolutionary process and had thus brought forward the question, "So far as man and his values

---

[1] William Paley, *Natural Theology* (1802).

are concerned, is the purpose of the world benevolent, malevolent, or indifferent?" The assumption that nature is indifferent or malevolent would create the problem of explaining the presence of goodness, truth, and beauty in the world. According to evolutionary theory, the existence of values, the apparent upward trend of evolution, and the adaptation of species to their environment can be adequately explained only through the hypothesis that God's intelligent guidance is responsible for progress in organic evolution, including the conservation of values, such as truth, moral good, and beauty. Alfred Lord Tennyson expressed this point of view in his verse:

> That God, which ever lives and loves,
> One God, one law, one element,
> And one far-off divine event,
> To which the whole creation moves.

The French philosopher Henri Bergson, who posited a life principle (the Elan Vital) in the universe, introduced a concept of flexibility in purpose in evolution. Bergson maintained that God operates with complete freedom in unfolding the process of evolution, that God, like an artist who works completely unrestricted by outside forces, freely chooses each new step of creative activity as he develops successive stages of the evolutionary process. The American philosopher C. Lloyd Morgan formulated a comparable *Theory of Emergent Evolution* in an effort to explain consciousness, self-awareness, and life as emergents, or new phenomena in the ongoing processes of natural evolution.

All such theorists emphasizing the concept of evolution assume a God who is immanent in the world, continuously active in the creative process, a point of view central to the religious philosophers of Theism and Pantheism.

The Ontological Argument. The basis for the Ontological Argument is the fact that the idea of a Supreme Being has always been a universal concept of mankind. Thus Saint Anselm of Canterbury (1033-1109), the most influential proponent of the Ontological Argument, set forth the following argument:

> We have a concept of a Perfect Being;
> Such a Perfect Being must necessarily exist.
> Why? If he did not exist, then he would not be perfect.

To quote Saint Anselm: "Assuredly that, than which nothing greater can be conceived, cannot exist in the understanding alone. For, suppose it exists in the understanding alone: then it can be conceived to exist in reality; which is greater. Therefore, if that, than which nothing greater can be conceived, exists in the understanding alone, the very being, than which nothing greater can be conceived, is one, than which a greater can be conceived. But obviously this is impossible. Hence there is no doubt that there exists a being, than which nothing greater can be conceived, and it exists both in the understanding and in reality." [1]

Saint Anselm here maintains that the existence of God must be deduced from his attribute of perfection. Other religious philosophers have preferred to emphasize the idea that the characteristic quality of a perfect Being is indicated by the subsistent nature of perfect relationships in mathematics, logic, and other sciences.

It is true that we have a concept of perfection evidenced by mathematical concepts, but to ascribe existence to them is unwarranted, for unlike the *ex*istence of human beings and physical nature, they *sub*sist. If the concept of God is accepted as a principle, then it may be concluded that he subsists, but will a subsistent God be satisfactory to Theists? Probably not.

The monk Gaunilo, a contemporary of Saint Anselm, repudiated the Ontological Argument, arguing that a person could prove the existence of a nonexistent island by asserting that he had an idea of a perfect island. From Saint Anselm's point of view, however, Gaunilo was mistaken in assuming that such an island is a genuine concept, whereas it is merely an imaginary phenomenon; to Saint Anselm God is a non-phenomenal (noumenal) concept, as shown by its universality among human beings, so that consequently his existence (or preferably subsistence) follows necessarily.

Decartes also developed an Ontological Argument for God's existence. He asserted that we have innately imbedded in our minds the idea of God, an infinite Being, yet we are neither infinite nor did we receive this idea from experience (since we can-

---

[1] Saint Anselm, *Proslogium,* tr. S. W. Deane (LaSalle, Illinois: Open Court Publishing Co., 1903).

not sense God). Accordingly, said Descartes, the idea must have issued from the Infinite himself, who must of necessity exist. "For though the idea of substance be in my mind owing to this, that I myself am a substance, I should not, however, have the idea of an infinite substance, seeing I am a finite being, unless it were given me by some substance in reality infinite." [1]

The principal objection to the Cartesian Ontological Argument is its predication of God on the basis of an idea of him, assuming his existence on the ground of a mere conceptual definition. Nevertheless, the contention that the idea of God is innate has always posed a problem; in contemporary times, this idea has been widely accepted among various religious groups. The fact that each instinct finds its counterpart in life (e.g., the instinct of thirst finds its complement in water, that of hunger in food) is put forward as evidence that the instinctive belief in God proves his existence. This argument derives a measure of support from those sociologists who attest that man in all societies has practiced some form of religion, that hence religion must be considered to be a universal culture trait or instinct.

The Axiological Argument. The fact that there are moral values in the world provides the basis for the Axiological Argument, which states that if God did not exist such values would be inexplicable or irrational. There are two forms of the Axiological Argument, namely, the Moral Argument and the Argument from Values.

The Moral Argument. Every person experiences the necessity for making moral choices and senses his moral obligations in the light of actual ideals. The Moral Argument holds that such universality of moral conscience can be explained more logically on the assumption of the existence of a moral deity, God, than it can on the basis of atheistic beliefs. Although men differ as to precisely what is moral, they nevertheless do face life in a moral light, as moral beings; consequently, moral ideals and moral existence are real and, being real, can be explained logically by assuming the existence of a moral God.

The Argument from Values (the Axiological Argument). Not

---

[1] René Descartes, *Meditations,* tr. John Veitch (original French version, 1641).

only man's experience but the world as a whole indicates the presence of moral values. Truth, beauty, and goodness not only are experienced within the individual's subjective consciousness but also are sensed as external realities. The human being's awareness of moral values implies their objective existence. Even conflicting subjective interpretations of truth, beauty, and goodness presuppose or tacitly indicate an Absolute Value, the Supreme Value (God).

The Religio-Empirical Argument. The argument from religious experience, the Religio-Empirical Argument, asserts that since our knowledge of the world is based on experience, then religious experience like all other forms of experience must be accorded validity. The fact that religious beliefs have been found in all societies, ancient and modern, primitive and civilized, is taken as evidence of their basis in reality.

William James argued that since all normal persons have religious experiences, and since experience is their criterion of truth, then God, the object of their religious experience, must be (like the objects of all their other experiences) factually true.[1] Furthermore, said James, inasmuch as a person's experience of God does make a practical difference in living, the Pragmatic test of truth corroborates the assumption that God exists.

The cogency of the Religio-Empirical Argument is indeed enhanced by the remarkable consequences attributed to religious experiences. The idea of God has been so potent as to alter not only the lives of individual men but also the course of all history, for throughout history societies have been changed by religious experiences. If the experiences of religious men were to be deleted from the annals of the history of civilization, the record would exclude the world's best achievements and most precious ingredients. Consider to what extent the world's destiny has been molded by religious mystics and saints, such as Moses, Socrates, Jesus, Luther, Buddha, and Gandhi. Consider the heights to which religious experience has inspired men of literature, art, sculpture, architecture, and music. The idea of God harmonizes and enhances an orderly, purposeful, moral world, renders it

---

[1] William James, *Varieties of Religious Experience.*

more meaningful, giving man a cause for which to live, as well as his inspiration for living. The Religio-Empirical Argument states that it is much more reasonable to posit an existent God as the basis for religious experience than to attribute the extraordinary consequences of religion to belief in a mere fairy tale or imaginary deity.

The Epistemological Argument. The principal basis for the Epistemological Argument is the view that the world is meaningful and rational, therefore inconceivable without a Supreme Source, namely, the creative, controlling mind of God which gives it order and purpose. Only within an ordered, meaningful universe could science derive truths verifiable through experience. Haphazard objects and events could never account for an orderly system of natural laws, and one must assume that, since man does not simply invent or imagine a meaningful universe, a Supreme Mind, God, endows it with meaning.

This argument may be illustrated by analogy with Shakespeare's *Hamlet*. Would it be reasonable to suppose that the Shakespearean play resulted from the haphazard scattering of many pieces of printer's type? Is it not obvious that a mind carefully arranged it, imputing meaning to it? By the same line of reasoning, it would be fantastic to the point of absurdity to conclude that the world's order and meaning were created by accident. (The distinction between the Epistemological Argument and the comparable Teleological Argument is that, whereas the former is based on the concept of world order and purpose, the latter emphasizes order and meaning as governing forces in the universe.)

The Anthropological Argument. According to the Anthropological Argument, God's existence must be assumed from the nature of man—his ability to think logically, mathematically, symbolically, scientifically, rhetorically, abstractly; his ability to appreciate and create works of art, such as those of music, sculpture, and painting; his sense of humor, his moral insight, and his religious insight. These significant and distinctive attributes of human personality must be accepted as evidence of a Supreme Mind, which not only encompasses and surpasses all powers of the human intellect but also serves as their source or creator, indeed the source and creator of man himself. In this sense, man is said to have been created in the image of God.

AGNOSTICISM AND ATHEISM

Agnostics join the Atheists in contesting the traditional arguments which purport to prove the existence of God. The Agnostic offers a non-committed view in contrast to the dogmatic negativism of the Atheists.

Agnosticism.   The term *Agnosticism* (coined by Thomas Henry Huxley, 1825-1895) refers to a neutralist view on the question of the existence of God; it is the view of the person who elects to remain in a state of suspended judgment. One group of Agnostics assumes that it merely lacks the facts necessary to form a judgment and defers any conclusion pending the acquisition of such facts; another group assumes a more dogmatic position, contending that facts are not available because it is impossible now (and will continue to be impossible) to obtain these facts—a view exemplified in Immanuel Kant's attacks upon the traditional arguments for the existence of God. Among foremost Agnostics are T. H. Huxley, Immanuel Kant, Charles Darwin, and Bertrand Russell.

Atheism.   Unlike Agnostics, the Atheist takes a definite stand, arguing that proof regarding God's existence or nonexistence is available, but that the evidence favors the assumption of nonexistence. (In fact, the Theists, Agnostics, and Atheists can all become quite dogmatic, with Theists insistent they can prove God's existence, Atheists equally certain they can prove that God does not exist, and most Agnostics perfectly confident they can prove knowledge of God to be impossible. Thus, individuals are left to decide this issue for themselves in the light of available facts, and many will tend to accept the most inclusive, the most coherent, position.)

Noted adherents of Atheism include Sigmund Freud, George Santayana, Karl Marx, and Jean-Paul Sartre.

The Universe as Chaotic.   Perhaps the strongest argument of the Atheists is that the world behaves in a chaotic, meaningless, irrational way. Shakespeare's Macbeth expresses this view when the future appears desperate, meaningless, chaotic:

> To-morrow, and to-morrow, and tomorrow,
> Creeps in this petty pace from day to day,
> To the last syllable of recorded time;
> And all our yesterdays have lighted fools
> The way to dusty death. Out, out, brief candle!
> Life's but a walking shadow; a poor player,
> That struts and frets his hour upon the stage,
> And then is heard no more: *it is a tale*
> Told by an idiot, full of *sound and fury,*
> *Signifying nothing.*
>
> (*Macbeth*, Act V, Scene 5)

(Shakespeare's own conclusions, however, cannot be deduced from the emotional utterances of his characters.) Among contemporary schools of philosophy, none, with the possible exception of a few Existentialists, accepts the Atheists' argument that the world is meaningless; and none of the system-building philosophers in modern times (except the Pessimist Schopenhauer) has attempted to use the argument as a defense of Atheism. Perhaps the reason for this is that most Atheists in the academic world like to think themselves scientific, and some even fancy themselves as guardians of science as if they were protecting it from the onslaught of religious institutions and persons who might threaten its progress. Science is predicated on the fact that the world is rich in meaning, at least enough meaning to make possible the derivation of scientific laws. To assert that the world is meaningless is to claim that it is incapable of being interpreted by means of science, and that hence it would be impossible for man to derive scientific laws from the facts of nature. Thus, both for the religious philosopher and for the scientist, the person in question would lose all sense of direction, value, and will for living; such a view would render life futile and encourage suicidal tendencies. This reasoning brings us back to the Epistemological Argument based on the principle that any meaning in life and the world must be attributed to God, the Supreme Mind infusing the universe.

The Argument from Fear. Sigmund Freud and Bertrand Russell, among other leading modern philosophers, have asserted that man's interest in religions is based on fear—that fear of the unknown, fear of the uncontrollable, fear of nature, drives man to religion, to a God deemed capable of controlling nature so that, when danger threatens, man will be protected from dread objects and events. According to this argument, religion was spawned in fear, superstition, and ignorance; and fear of the unknown, at a time of ignorance concerning scientific causes, drove man to superstition.

Logicians criticize the preceding argument as an example of a *genetic fallacy,* the error of assuming that a point has been proved merely because it has been traced to its source. It may be of interest, and definitely is of interest to at least the psychologist and the historian, to ascertain how our religious beliefs emerged and what gave them their initial impetus, but so far as proof of Atheism is concerned, such factors are irrelevant. Thus, evidence that a particular science grew out of magic or alchemy does not imply that science today is invalid.

The Argument from Evolution.   It has been assumed by some that the existence of God is an unnecessary hypothesis because the theory of evolution explains the generation of life and that the concept of the survival of the fittest explains design in the universe. But some religious philosophers (e.g., Borden Parker Bowne) point out that the theory of evolution merely describes the development of life and is quite consistent with a Deistic conclusion. In fact, they say, the theory can be used to defend the thesis that evolutionary processes indicate God's existence and are clarified by appeal to such a hypothesis. In this sense, the theory of evolution is merely a generalization describing God's creative handiwork.

The Anthropomorphic Argument.   The main thesis of the Anthropomorphic Argument was stated as follows by the ancient Greek philosopher Xenophanes (*c.* 570-475 B.C.): "Ethiopians make their gods black and snub-nosed; Thracians give theirs blue eyes and red hair. Yet if oxen and lions had hands, and could paint with their hands, and fashion images, as men do, they would make the pictures and images of their gods in their own likeness; horses would make them like horses, and oxen like oxen." [1] Sim-

---

[1] *Source Book in Ancient Philosophy,* Charles M. Bakewell, ed. (New York: Charles Scribner's Sons, 1907), p. 8.

ilarly, modern Atheists reverse the biblical statement that God
made man in his own image, asserting that man makes God in
his own image. They assume that God is merely the projection
of man's mind, a product of his imagination.

The Anthropomorphic Argument, which ascribes human qualities to nonhuman beings, does not justify comparable attribution
of personal qualities to a nonhuman personal entity. The Theists
take it for granted that God is personal but not anthropomorphic.
From their standpoint, the Atheist's attempt to depersonalize the
universe must fail, for knowledge possessed by the human mind
becomes immediately personal even if it refers to superhuman
verities.

Who Made God? In rejoinder to the Etiological Argument
which purports to prove the existence of God on the basis of a
First Cause, Atheists ask, "If God made all things, then who made
God?" This provocative question, however, has no logical validity, for it involves the fallacy known as *compound questions*. Its
wording implies a contradiction or logical dilemma; it is analogous to the question, "Have you stopped beating your wife?" in
which either answer, *Yes* or *No,* is self-incriminating (even
though these are the only permissible answers) because of the
implications inherent in the question. Thus, the question, "Who
made God?" assumes that the creation of God is a proven fact
which justifies the search for God's maker. Furthermore, the antecedent to the pronoun *who* is lacking; if the antecedent is God,
then the conclusion would be that "God made God"; if the antecedent is not God, then the Being in question must be God, while
the second God must be an imposter, a creature, not Creator.
Thus the question "Who made God?" involves a logical fallacy,
which cannot be accepted as a basis for denying the existence of
God.

The Argument from Naive Realism. According to the philosophy of Naive Realism, all things are as they appear to the senses,
and nothing beyond sense experience exists. Since God cannot
be experienced by means of sense modalities, he does not exist
but is merely a mythical creation of the human mind.

The major premise of Naive Realism is not, however, a valid
basis for such a conclusion. Not only does it assume what is yet

to be proved (that all truths must be derived from sense experience) but it is also contrary to established scientific evidence. For example, as previously noted, sense experience would compel us to assume that a straight stick bends in water—even though this illusion is contradicted by experimental proof. Moreover, the inadequacy of sensory experience as such is quite apparent from the fact that many natural entities, such as light waves and atomic particles, cannot be detected by means of the unaided sensory apparatus. And what could be more trustworthy as a criterion of truth than the relationships of logic and mathematics, generally beyond mere sense perception?

THE SOUL

The following traditional theories have become prominent in the history of religious philosophy: (1) *Epiphenomenalism* denies any independent reality to the soul, assuming that the soul is merely a by-product of the biological organism and perishes with the demise of the body. (2) *Interactionism* ascribes separate, though in some respects interdependent, reality to both soul and body; neither is merely an offshoot of the other, though one may affect the other. (3) *Substantialism* depicts man as triadic, possessing a soul, a mind, and a body.

Epiphenomenalism. The Epiphenomenal view, which refuses to ascribe real existence to mind or soul, considers the body to be the only reality; mind and soul are epiphenomena (i.e., transitory and ephemeral by-products, offshoots, or functions of the physical body) whose existence continues only as long as the body lives. Since this view reduces the mind and soul to the status of merely physical entities, it has been termed *Reductionism*.

The main thesis of Epiphenomenalism derives support from Behavioristic psychology propounded by John B. Watson and other modern psychologists. Behaviorists assume that the only scientific and valid approach to mental or psychological phenomena is visible and measurable behavior, reduce all mental activity to stimulus-response mechanisms, biological or physiological in nature, and conclude that only the physical body exists ultimately, not soul or mind which are merely bodily functions. Epiphenomenalism rejects all possibility of future life; it excludes immortality from all discussion as a mythical entity having no chance of being true.

Interactionism. The belief that body and mind are equally real is accepted by the Interactionist, who uses the terms *mind* and *soul* interchangeably. The Interactionist rejects the Epiphenomenalist claim that mind is the mere outgrowth of the body and points out that the mind is capable of affecting the body as dramatically as the body affects the mind. Sigmund Freud and Carl Jung have proved that the mind does affect the body profoundly, often so much as to cause serious physical illness. Contemporary psychosomatic medicine attests to the sizable number of ailments resulting from disturbances within the mind: e.g., ulcers, heart disease, rheumatoid arthritis. Evidence that the mind affects the body supports the Interactionist claims against Epiphenomenalism. The line of reasoning used by Epiphenomenalism is turned against it. If the fact that the body affects the mind indicates that the mind as such does not exist as a separate entity, then the fact that the mind affects the body should similarly indicate that the body is not ultimately real.

Substantialism. The view of man as triune (possessing a body, a mind, and a soul), or *Substantialism,* has been accepted among Neo-Thomists, Roman Catholics, and certain non-Catholic religious philosophers such as Borden Parker Bowne. Adherents make a clear distinction between body, mind, and soul; they believe that man has a body (which includes the brain), and mind (which accounts for the rest of his mental experiences, except those attributed to the soul), and a soul (which, as expounded by Saint Thomas Aquinas, is the principle governing man's reason). Bowne regards the soul as the unifying principle of the human mind. In contrast, Aquinas identifies man's intellectual self as supernal, as a *soul substance,* the intellectual immortal reality or spiritual self which constitutes a human characteristic most akin to God.

THE MIND-BODY PROBLEM

The mind-body problem has been one of the oldest and most persistent in the history of philosophy. It is a known fact, an obvious one, that the mind affects the body (worry causes ulcers) and the body affects the mind (alcohol causes mental disturbances). Although the interaction of body and mind may occur hundreds of times in a day, no philosopher, psychologist, or physicist has been able to determine where or how it occurs.

Metaphysical Dualism; Occasionalism. The French Rationalist René Descartes conceived of matter and mind (body and spirit) as two distinctly different and separate substances, each ultimately real in its own right. The fact that they function together in harmony presented a problem: How can two substances which possess nothing in common interact in harmony?

Descartes and his followers at first claimed that the pineal gland in the brain is the site of interaction between body and mind, but this conclusion received little credence and was abandoned. The Cartesians also attributed all interaction to the will of God, whose intervening activity created the required energy; thus the apparent multiple causes were unreal, and God is the only real cause of the interacting functions of body and mind. This view has been referred to as the doctrine of Occasionalism. The early Occasionalists, Arnold Geulincx and Nicole Malebranche, were not particularly influential in the history of modern philosophy. Nevertheless, it should be noted that some contemporary Personalist philosophers have incorporated Occasionalism into their system in modified form. The Personalist Albert Cornelius Knudson (1873-1953) declared that "Occasionalism thus finds itself in this respect in accord with the prevailing intellectual temper of the day. It does not see in every material thing the phenomenal manifestation of a soul. For if matter as such is de-animized, it is grounded directly in the divine activity, not in the activity of independent spirits." [1] In fact, ancient philosophers, including Aristotle, as well as modern philosophers, may be said to share to some extent in the attempt of the Occasionalists, to ascribe real causes to divine intervention.

Psychophysical Parallelism. The theory of Psychophysical Parallelism states that, although the mental and the physical realities do not interact, for every mental change there is a correspond-

---

[1] Albert C. Knudson, *The Philosophy of Personalism* (New York: The Abingdon Press, 1927).

ing physical change. In the words of Benedict Spinoza, the most influential proponent of this hypothesis, "the order and connection of ideas is the same as the order and connection of things." [1] Psychophysical Parallelism regards the mind-body relationship as analogous to a two-sided sheet of paper; since whatever happens to either side affects the sheet, anything that happens to the sheet affects both sides. Accordingly, whatever happens to mind will have its corresponding effect on the body and whatever happens to the body will have its concomitant effect on the mind.

Preëstablished Harmony. Gottfried Wilhelm Leibniz (1644-1716) formulated the theory that denied the reality of body-mind interaction, asserting that the apparent interaction reflected only a Preëstablished Harmony foreordained by God. In this view the mind and body operate *as if* they interact and *as if* each is aware of the other, but such interaction is only an illusion or appearance. The native (inherent) structure and nature of mind and matter are such that merely by functioning according to the prescribed nature of each, they produce a harmonious result that gives an impression of interaction. Leibniz's principle may be illustrated by analogy to the simultaneous working of five clocks set to indicate precisely the same time; although each maintains perfect unison with the others (giving the false impression of deliberate interaction), yet each is completely independent of the other. The principle of Preëstablished Harmony explains their functioning in concert.

Doctrine of Divine Arbitrariness. The British empiricist philosopher George Berkeley (1685-1753) asserted that although certain connections prevail among natural objects, these are not causal, and he denied the cause-effect relationship altogether. It was his view that the apparent interaction among events results, not from a necessary sequence of causes and their effects, but from the arbitrary will of God—hence his Doctrine of Divine Arbitrariness. "Not that there is any natural or necessary connexion." [2]

Panphenomenalism. David Hume (1711-1776) formulated the

---

[1] Benedict Spinoza, *Ethics* (1677, posthumously), Part II, Proposition 7.
[2] George Berkeley, *New Theory of Vision* (1709).

theory of Panphenomenalism. He denied the existence of all ultimate reality (metaphysical reality), accepting as valid data only those things experienced as sense impressions; in other words, he asserted that existence is limited to phenomena, which are objects, not of reason, but of experience. By rejecting the idea of *cause* and *soul* as substances, he eliminated the entire problem of interaction. Hume concluded that events depend upon merely repetitious or sequential activities; that nothing in the universe is ever created, or caused to act, by anything else; and that reality consists only of a series of phenomena appearing in a temporal order.

IMMORTALITY

Immortality, broadly defined as the survival of human personality beyond death, has been a universal concept in the history of mankind. Four major interpretations have been historically prominent: (1) the body continues after death by means of the deceased person's offspring (in some cultures, the continuation takes the form of physical preservation as mummies); (2) the eternal soul leaves its enshrined body to enter a new one (transmigration of soul); (3) the soul, being by nature eternal, survives bodily death; (4) the soul survives only under certain conditions usually prescribed by God, for its survival depends upon God's specific decision.

SPURIOUS FORMS OF IMMORTALITY

Substitutes for individual immortality have often served as a source of consolation for people unable to believe that the soul survives physical death. These substitute values, which may be regarded as spurious forms of individual immortality, are social immortality, biological immortality, and impersonal immortality.

Social Immortality. Some individuals feel that their good deeds will have an enduring influence long after they have died and consider that influence an adequate form of immortality, properly termed *social immortality,* or survival in the minds of other men. Is it not true that the words of leaders such as Jesus, Moses, Shakespeare, and Gandhi have given them a warm, permanent place in the hearts and minds of succeeding generations? In this sense, these men may be said to live on long after physical death.

Critics of this belief in social immortality point out, however, that after death the individual himself does not personally experience his immortal existence and derives no benefit from his ongoing influence, which hence might just as well have been contributed by anyone else so far as he is concerned. They also point out that good people may be quickly forgotten, while evil ones such as Nero and Hitler may find an enduring place in history—an infamous place, it is indeed true, yet one approaching social immortality.

Biological Immortality. Some people derive consolation from the belief that their progeny will survive and that each succeeding generation will extend their identification with history in an endless chain of immortality. This idea of biological immortality is accepted by them as an adequate substitute for the belief in individual immortality.

Nevertheless, those who find biological immortality unacceptable emphasize the fact that many virtuous people may have no children, whereas the descendants of Cain may constitute an infinite procession of pernicious influences. Moreover, the time will come when the earth and all its inhabitants will disappear, thus ending any hopes of biological immortality.

Impersonal Immortality. Belief in still another form of immortality has been common among Pantheists and others, who hold the view that life beyond death is not individual (personal), but corporate in the sense that all persons are fused into one Being (either in the Absolute, or in a state of Nirvana as the Hindus teach, or in universal mankind as Plato taught). This type of Impersonal or Pantheistic Immortality has failed to convince religious philosophers who value individual personality most of all and are willing to settle for nothing less than belief in the indestructibility of each human soul.

ARGUMENTS AGAINST IMMORTALITY

Among numerous historically prominent objections to the concept of individual immortality, the following arguments have been most persistently and frequently advanced.

Behaviorism. Behavioristic psychology has been made the basis for one of the most cogent arguments against the concept of personal immortality. Behaviorism, by reducing all mental phenomena to biological or physiological components, eliminates any need for postulating the metaphysical existence of the soul, and hence rejects the idea of spiritual immortality.

The Behavioristic Argument has been weakened by the fact that Behaviorism as a point of view in psychology is today not so firmly entrenched as it was some decades ago. In addition, psycho-analysis and psychosomatic medicine have emphasized the profound influence of mental experience upon the functions of the body. It would seem to be just as logical, therefore, to postulate an immortal mind that affects the body as it would be to assume with the Behaviorists that only the physical organism exists. In fact, it is a *post hoc* fallacy to conclude that a mere sequence in physical events proves there are physical instead of mental causes.

Wishful Thinking. There are those who reject the idea of immortality on the ground that it is merely a product of wishful thinking, an overoptimistic vision of an unreal ideal. Nevertheless, not all the optimistic hopes of mankind fall by the wayside. Some do come true, and who can be sure that the belief in immortality is not one of these? The miracle drugs were once regarded as impossible miracles, but they eventually proved themselves to be feasible and effective; so, too, zealous faith in spiritual immortality might be found consistent with reality.

Lowly Origin. It is claimed that the belief in immortality originated in the dreams of ignorant, primitive communities and hence is not entitled to serious consideration. In logic this reasoning is known as a *genetic fallacy,* for it assumes that an untutored source of a conclusion is evidence of its falsity. But true ideas may arise among the ignorant and humble, and one of these could be the concept of personal immortality.

Skepticism of Scientists. The assumption that most scientists reject the concept of immortality has sometimes been put forth as a decisive argument, but this assumption has never been proved and even if it were correct, we should bear in mind that scientists are not qualified to decide issues in the philosophy of religion. Such an argument is based on the fallacy of *misplaced authority* for the scientist lacks authoritative standing outside of his field of specialization.

Concept of Finite Series.   The Argument of Finite Series states that the idea of immortality cannot be accepted because whatever has a beginning must also have an ending. Nevertheless, some things, as in mathematics, do have a beginning without an ending—for example, an arithmetical series may begin with the number I and continue to infinity, or a line may begin at a given point and extend indefinitely.

ARGUMENTS FOR IMMORTALITY

The following arguments have induced many people to accept a belief in personal immortality or have helped to strengthen such a belief.

The Conservation of Values.   The religious philosopher Douglas Clyde Macintosh has eloquently defended the concept of immortality on the ground that only such an assumption could be consistent with a universe of values. If people should cease to exist, the spiritual values of truth, beauty, virtue, and love would perish; the survival of the good depends upon the survival of personality. Since God is infinite and immortal, so too are the values he has created, values which are found in persons, and which give to each personality its highest worth. Values and personality are the permanent handiwork of God, "a Power great enough and good enough to conserve the human individual in spite of bodily death." [1]

The sentiment of this argument is found delightfully expressed by Alfred Lord Tennyson:

> That nothing walks with aimless feet;
>   That not one life shall be destroy'd
>   Or cast as rubbish to the void,
> When God hath made the pile complete.
> *(In Memoriam)*

Note that the argument based on values depends upon two assumptions: the existence of God; and God's goodness.

---

[1] Douglas Clyde Macintosh, *The Reasonableness of Christianity* (New York: Charles Scribner's Sons, 1925), Ch. 4.

The Moral Argument. The noted German philosopher Immanuel Kant and the British religious philosopher Frederick Robert Tennant were among the most influential adherents of the Moral Argument for the concept of immortality. This argument is based upon the righteousness of God, reflected in the query, "The requiter of justice shall he not do what is right?"

The Moral Argument has several versions, one of which states that God has given man a moral task which requires more than one lifetime to accomplish. Since God is just, he will assure man the necessary eternal life to fulfill his obligations.

Another version of the Moral Argument postulates that immortality is essential in order to "right the wrongs" suffered in this present life.

A third version of the Moral Argument (one which Tennant emphasized) states that immortality is necessary to fulfill the purpose of the world, namely, the development of virtuous people who will be granted a future life so that they may achieve their moral goals (for only man is conscious of his impending death and the possibility of immortal life); if God is good, he will not deceive people but will, on the contrary, provide them with continuing life after physical death in order to accomplish God's purposes.

Note that these arguments depend upon the assumption that a beneficent God exists. In the words of Edgar Sheffield Brightman, "It is unthinkable that the purpose of the universe should fail. . . . If there be a God, man's immortality is certain; if not, immortality would not be worth having." [1]

The Argument from Analogy. The eighteenth-century British philosopher Joseph Butler postulated that a life beyond death is a genuine possibility on the basis of an analogy between the changing life form of a caterpillar and a potentially new form of human existence after death. He pointed out that if a metamorphosis from caterpillar to butterfly is but a natural process, surely the higher species, man, should be granted the possibility of a postmortem form of existence.

---

[1] Edgar S. Brightman, *An Introduction to Philosophy* (New York: Henry Holt and Co., 1925), pp. 349, 351.

The Transmission Theory. In his defense of the concept of personal immortality, William James distinguished between "productive" and "transmissive" functions of man. According to James, the physical body does not produce the mind, but merely transmits mental functions; that is to say, the mind expresses itself through the body. Immortality, then, is a state in which the veil (the body) has been removed so that the soul achieves full freedom without the necessity of using the mortal instrument, the physical body.

Universality of Belief. The argument that since the belief in personal immortality is universal, it should be accepted as true is subject to logical and factual objections. Universality of belief must be distinguished from validity, for mankind has often throughout history accepted incorrect concepts until these were eventually disproved. Belief in immortality is far short of being universal, and many people have been either dubious about or antagonistic to such a conclusion. It would be quite easy to hold that immortality is only a myth, or an idea reflecting the wishful thinking of its adherents.

THE PROBLEM OF EVIL

In the philosophy of religion, the problem of evil relates more fundamentally to the nature of the universe than it does to the moral conduct of mankind. Moral evil in society depends chiefly on the individual's choice among alternative courses of action, whereas evil attributed to natural forces is beyond human control and raises the question of superhuman responsibility. The principal views concerning the moral nature of the universe are those of Optimism, Pessimism, and Meliorism.

Optimism. Adherents of Optimism agree with Browning that "God's in his heaven: All's right with the world" [1] and assume that nature, being the work of an omnipotent good God, is necessarily ordered for the best, or at least is essentially arranged to achieve the highest good.

The eminent German philosopher Gottfried Wilhelm Leibniz argued that the existing universe must be the best of all possible

---

[1] Robert Browning, *Pippa Passes.*

worlds because a perfectly beneficent God would desire only the best world, an omniscient God would know which was the best world, and an omnipotent God would tolerate only the best possible world. Leibniz explained that so-called "evils," including doubts and unsolved problems, are inevitable ingredients of a world such as ours, that such "evils" are necessary in order to make possible the contrasting good values of high intelligence, freedom of will, and other desirable aspects of this best of all worlds.

Benedict Spinoza, the great philosopher known as the "God-intoxicated"[1] man, arrived at the same view of the world as the perfect expression of a good God, stating further that the world is in fact identical with God (Pantheism). He equated the idea of evil with ignorance, the inability to see reality from God's perspective; to Spinoza, evil reflected only a lack of understanding, an incoherent view of reality, an integration which distorts the correct arrangement of facts.

Pessimism. Adherents of Pessimism hold the view that the universe is indifferent to value, or, worse still, hostile to value and therefore characterized by evil rather than good. Some of them regard evil as relatively more prevalent than good, while others consider life itself to be essentially painful, hence not worth living.

Rather than leading to belief in a good God, or any God whatever, Pessimism normally implies Atheism. Pessimism which views the world as hostile to value tends to Pan-Satanism, the belief that the world expresses Satan's personality. Pan-Satanism is incapable of explaining the presence of *good* in the world.

Pessimists believe in *surd* or *dysteleological* evil, which serves no good purpose whatever and is not instrumental to a good end. Ernst Haeckel coined the term *dysteleology* to depict nature as purposeless. The classic systematic philosophy of Arthur Schopenhauer portrayed reality as blind force (will). A noteworthy contemporary Pessimist, the Existentialist Martin Heidegger, describes reality as anxiety, nothingness, and death. Bert-

---

[1] The philosopher Novalis attached this epithet to Spinoza.

rand Russell is another contemporary philosopher who holds that the world is indifferent to value.

Meliorism. The Meliorists believe that the world is progressively improving and that man can contribute to its enhancement. Thus Herbert Spencer and Edgar S. Brightman regarded the good in the world as dominant over evil. In Brightman's view, the world is steadily regenerating through the co-operative efforts of God and man directed toward infinite perfectibility.

PART FIVE—METAPHYSICS

PART FIVE—METAPHYSICS

The term *metaphysics* is derived from the Greek *meta ta phu-sika* (meaning after or beyond physical nature). Metaphysics refers to the study of ultimate reality, that is, the study of what transcends physical things.

Objects which manifest themselves to the senses are phenomenal; consequently, philosophers distinguish between phenomenal existence (the object as it appears to the senses) and metaphysical reality (the object as it truly or ultimately is). For example, a glass of water appears to be fluid, wet, and colorless, but in reality it consists of two parts hydrogen to one part oxygen The real water (the two atoms of hydrogen and one atom of oxygen) is not apparent to the senses, which picture water as fluid, wet, and colorless, while the phenomenal is. Metaphysics studies this relationship between reality and appearance in an effort to describe the fundamental nature of the universe.[1]

Aristotelian Definition. An ancient tradition held that the term metaphysics merely signified the arrangement of books in Aristotle's library. Since the books treating metaphysics appeared after those dealing with physics, they were known as *meta physics* (after physics). This tradition has been passed down to us by Andronicus of Rhodes, who edited the writings of Aristotle, arranged them in an order accepted thereafter, and himself probably coined the term *metaphysics*.

The metaphysical writings of Aristotle contained his *First Philosophy* (natural theology), dealing with the existence of God, the nature of being, causation, etc. These writings transcend physical or phenomenal experience and consider ultimate reality —the subject matter of metaphysics.

Traditional Branches of Metaphysics. Traditionally, meta-

---

[1] See Francis Herbert Bradley's classic work, *Appearance and Reality* (1891).

physics has been divided into four major branches, first delineated by Christian Wolff, the notable German systematizer of Leibnizian philosophy: (1) *ontology*, the study of ultimate Being, (2) *cosmology*, the study of the ultimate order of the universe, (3) *psychology*, that is, rational psychology or evaluative psychology as opposed to current scientific empirical psychology, and (4) *natural theology*, the study of the nature and existence of God to the extent that it is possible to detect him from the empirical facts of nature and reason.

Epistemology, the study of how man obtains knowledge, has also been included as a subdivision of metaphysics by some great philosophers; Georg Hegel, for example, equated it with logic, and he designated the real as the rational and the rational as the real. John Stuart Mill referred to metaphysics as "that portion of mental philosophy which attempts to determine what part of the furniture of the mind belongs to it originally, and what part is constructed out of materials furnished to it from without." Immanuel Kant relegated metaphysics to the area which transcends human experience, hence is beyond the reach of legitimate knowledge. The area of metaphysics was for him the realm of the unknowable, leaving the phenomenal world as the only genuinely knowable. He argued that valid knowledge cannot be gained concerning God, soul, immortality, etc. Thus Kant opened the door to Phenomenalism and Positivism. Schopenhauer associated metaphysics with experience, emphasizing analysis of the empirical or phenomenal facts of experience.

Pragmatists, who regard any discussions of ultimate reality as a sterile endeavor, are concerned only with the practical, utilitarian topics of philosophy. Many are in sympathy with William James' reference to metaphysics: "As in the night all cats are gray, so in the darkness of *metaphysical* criticism all causes are obscure."

On a historical basis metaphysics may be divided into Pre-Cartesian, originating with the ancient Greek philosophers; and Post-Cartesian (or modern metaphysics, since René Descartes is considered the father of modern metaphysics, and even of modern philosophy). The remainder of this discussion of metaphysics will make use of this historical or developmental approach.

PRE-CARTESIAN METAPHYSICS

Pre-Cartesian metaphysics in the Western world may be traced back to the Ionian physicists (during the period 600-528 B.C.), a triad of pre-Socratic Greek philosophers from Miletus who were concerned with the *problem of matter:* Thales (624-546 B.C.), Anaximander (610-546 B.C.), and Anaximenes (585-528 B.C.).

Ideas of the Milesian Philosophers. The Milesian philosophers were in search of *Being,* the stuff of which the world was composed, cosmic matter, that is to say, ultimate or metaphysical reality (ontologically real substance). Since these men were pioneers in such philosophical or scientific endeavor, it is only natural that their findings, and the language used to express them, were primitive.

Thales identified ultimate reality as water, for water is found in three states of matter: solid, liquid, and gas. Anaximenes declared it to be air, probably influenced by the importance, necessity, and changeability of air. Both water and air are vital necessities for existence. The Cosmologists ascribed life to matter, regarding it as animated, requiring air and water; such doctrines are termed *Hylozoism* (living matter). Anaximander, unlike Thales and Anaximenes, accepted a spaceless (infinite) and timeless (eternal) quality termed *apeiron* as the primary substance. The *apeiron* is cosmic matter which he described as *The Infinite, The Boundless, The Unlimited,* or *The Divine.*

The Eleatics. The Eleatic School adopted the view of its four leading philosophers from Elea: Xenophanes, with a theological basis; Parmenides, with a metaphysical emphasis; Zeno, with a dialectical approach; and Melissus, with arguments for the principle of the Infinite. The Eleatics (540 to 340 B.C.) were interested in the problem of identity and change, concluding that reality, being one, eliminates any possibility that change is genuinely or ultimately real.

The Eleatic Xenophanes, a critic of anthropomorphism (its role in Polytheism was particularly objectionable to him) introduced the idea of Monotheism into philosophy. The oneness of God he concluded from the diversities of nature functioning harmoniously together; furthermore, he identified this infinite, eternal, existence of the world with God—Pantheism.

The leader of the Eleatic School, Parmenides, developed a conception of the ontologically real—*Being*. He identified *thought* with Being; each is interchangeable with the other. Logically, what cannot be thought, cannot exist; thought is a prerequisite to existence. While existence or Being is the content of thought, thought is the form or principle of Being (existence). Being is anything that exists, that is corporeal, that occupies space, and hence empty space is meaningless, nothing, nonexistence. Parmenides argued that, inasmuch as empty space, or the void, is unreal, it follows that motion cannot exist, for motion, to be real, must move into unoccupied space or into *nothingness* which does not exist. Furthermore, plural or multiple objects differing from one another cannot exist, for this would imply their separation by empty space, an impossibility. So, Parmenides concluded, ultimate reality (Being) is one (in number and kind), eternal (there was no beginning to its existence), imperishable (everlasting), but *limited*.

Zeno of Elea, whom Aristotle credited as inventor of the *dialectic* method of reasoning, is known for his ability to refute the arguments of his opponents by reducing them to absurdities and contradictions. His classic arguments negate the reality of motion. One argument to prove the impossibility of motion cites the example of a flying arrow which is at rest at each given moment of time and therefore never moves. A comparable argument today might give the example of a moving object being photographed by a high-speed camera which actually can show us only a series of still pictures.

It was Melissus who contributed to the Eleatic School the idea of Being as *infinite*, for he argued that if space is limited, then it must be limited by empty space—which does not exist. Melissus, in effect, raised the question: "If space ends at a given point, then what could possibly be on the other side? More space?"

Heraclitus of Ephesus (544-484 B.C.) formulated a point of view antithetical to that of the Eleatics. His antithesis to the Eleatic thesis (*all is one, change is nonexistent*) stated that all is change (nothing abides, all things are in ceaseless change, in evolution; as the waters of a river are in a constant state of flux, ceaselessly flowing to the sea, so is all reality). Heraclitus made change "lord of the universe," insisting that nothing remains the same during any given period of two or more moments, but is constantly altering. Motion is at the base of all things; reality is a process; and thus, not *Being*, but *Becoming* is the nature of ultimate or metaphysical reality.

Becoming is best exemplified by the nature of fire, which is ever living, ever moving, never constant, always changing; therefore, said Heraclitus, fire must be the essence of all things. Nature, which is rhythmical and orderly, respects uniformity and law; hence, natural law—the *Logos* (reason or logic of the universe)— is the only permanent reality.

Eventually, the clash between the Eleatic thesis (of the *one as changeless*) and the Heraclitian antithesis (of all things in ceaseless change) was resolved by the synthesis of the Pluralists, who concluded that *Being is both identity and change*. Among the great Pluralists were Empedocles of Agrigentum in Sicily; Anaxagoras of Clazomene; and the two *Atomists* Leucippus and Democritus, both of Abdera. The Pluralists made their chief contributions to philosophy during the fifth century B.C. (*c.* 470 to 370 B.C.).

Empedocles. The first great Pluralist, Empedocles, postulated four basic elements, namely, earth, air, fire, and water, each of them imperishable, homogeneous, unchangeable, without any beginning, yet each divisible into smaller segments capable of change and movement. Although each object is subject to change, none contains within itself the cause of its motion; the cause is that external principle referred to by Empedocles as *love* and *hate*. Love and hate are powers, not mere feelings, functions, or relations.

Anaxagoras. The next great Pluralist, Anaxagoras, postulated a universe of innumerable elements. He assumed that every object in nature contains the elements and merely differs from other objects in form, color, and taste. These objects affect our senses to reveal their dominant sense properties which identify them individually. (For example, the properties white, granule, and sweetness identify sugar.) Anaxagoras believed that a principle which he called *Nous* (mind) gave the eternal, unchangeable elements the capacity of motion. Like the Eleatics, he pictured the elements as everlasting and concluded that they are immutable, thus formulating the *Doctrine of the Indestructibility of Matter*. He attributed the order, beauty, purpose, law, and harmony of the universe to *Nous,* which, as Reason, Mind, or Thought, he considered to be identical with Deity and to be the animating principle creating motion and causing all things to exist. With Anaxagoras, philosophy in this way introduced the concept of a teleological (purposive) explanation of the world.

Leucippus. The third noted Pluralist, Leucippus, contributed the concept of *atoms* (the uncuttable), elements which he portrayed as eternal, unchangeable, indestructible, homogeneous, indivisible, limited, but without a beginning in time. These innumerable atoms, filling infinite space, differ from one another in size, form, and location—in other words, only in quantitative respects. According to Leucippus, change of any kind in the universe starts with a shift in the position of *atoms in space.* Motion is therefore the consequence of reorganization among atoms and space relationships—the sole metaphysical realities.

Democritus. The fourth and most eminent of the Pluralists was the Atomist Democritus, regarded as the father of Materialism, who anticipated two modern principles of physics: (1) the Indestructibility of Matter, and (2) the Conservation of Energy. He maintained that nothing comes into being nor perishes in any absolute sense, for the indestructible atoms of which all things are made merely undergo a change in their order or arrangement.

Democritus held that fixed and necessary laws govern the behavior of atoms, which are themselves eternal, uncaused, and ever in motion, and hence, that motion, too, is eternal. In his view the world is not activated or put into order by means of any fortuitous concourse of atoms, but is governed mechanically by laws.

A mediating position between preceding philosophers, which consisted of a point of view based on the concept of number, was developed by Pythagoras of Samos (d. *c.* 497 B.C.) and his followers, particularly Philolaus of Thebes (a contemporary of Socrates). The mathematical idea of number was endowed with the qualities of the ultimate, metaphysical reality—permanence, immutability, imperishable universal validity, all these qualities being un-affected by time or change. According to the Pythagoreans the abiding essence of the world is to be found in mathematics, which gives shape or form to corporeal bodies; consequently, the Being of physical reality must consist of mathematical forms, and the world must be regarded as a harmony of numbers. The supreme value in the universe is something unchangeable, a per-manent value found only in the mathematical formula governing all things that exist.

The outstanding Sophist, Protagoras of Abdera (fifth century B.C.), advanced a *Perception Theory of Epistemology,* which re-duced the entire mental life of the individual to perceptions, to a *Sensualism* expressed in his dictum, "Man is the measure of all things." To Protagoras, knowledge, truth, and reality possess only a subjective existence, for they are merely opinions in each per-son's mind. There are no objective facts, no real truths binding on all people. What seems true for me is true only for me, and what seems true to you is true only for you. Since objectivity cannot be achieved, man must be content with subjective know-ledge or mere opinion.

The Sophist Gorgias (d. 380 B.C.) carried Protagoras' position to its ultimate conclusion of *Nihilism,* the belief that there is no ultimate reality, no metaphysical Being. Beyond human percep-tion, said Gorgias, there is no real substance (ontological being).

Not until the work of Plato (d. 347 B.C.) was a successful effort made to counteract the views of the Sophists and to restore a degree of validity to concepts of knowledge and reality.

Plato. Plato developed a new metaphysics (based in part on the ideas of Democritus) predicated on two different epistemolo-gies (systems of knowledge), each with its accompanying meta-physic (theory of reality or ultimate substance). According to Plato, human perception reveals phenomena as transient or rela-tive surface reality, whereas reason detects an absolute, perma-nent, universal, homogeneous reality or real laws of nature. The changing facts of phenomenal existence we perceive (sense), but the principles of reality we conceive (think). Sensory objects exist in the perceptual world, while the principles of reality exist in the metaphysical world of thought.

The latter world of metaphysical reality, the world known solely by the understanding, not perception, is the realm of Platonic Ideas. These ideas are principles, forms of true reality, ultimate Being itself, the knowledge of which is virtue. Ideas are incorporeal, for ultimate reality is beyond the physical; entirely devoid of phenomenal existence, they possess conceptual Being; they transcend phenomenal existence, and consequently they subsist. Lacking appearance, they must be understood; like mathematical principles, they have no sensory content, but must be comprehended through reason. Thus Plato's Doctrine of Ideas indicates the composition of the real world to be immaterial, incorporeal, ideal, hence, the core doctrine of *Platonic Idealism*.

Aristotle.   Aristotle attempted to solve the problem of identity and change, the central problem of Plato's two interacting worlds. He postulated a process of development which in his view conjoined the changing multiplicity of the phenomenal world with the unitary abiding Being of the metaphysically real world of Ideas.

To Aristotle, metaphysical reality is an *essence* which is itself inherent in phenomena; the potential or purpose (entelechy) of a phenomenal object makes it capable of realizing itself. Phenomenal existence is not real at its inception, but requires realization; to be actual is a process, one of self-actualization. The Being of a thing, the principles which govern it, its nature, are part of the phenomenal whole as realized. The universal is in the particular. Being therefore is the essence of an object which needs to be actualized, fully realized.

Plato's Ideas, said Aristotle, exist as *form,* while phenomena exist as matter; but, unlike Plato, Aristotle never allowed these two things to be separated. Form and matter are united permanently as *formed matter*. Without form, matter cannot be realized, and jointly form and matter constitute the combined phenomenal and real world, the world of existence. While nature produces only Being, *entelechy* transforms essence into full reality, actuality. Entelechy is the self-realization process of essence as it transpires from mere potential to actual reality.

According to Aristotle, the realization process of the essence in phenomena (that is to say, entelechy or the unfolding of reality) is effected in four ways. These ways or causes he classified as *material, formal, efficient,* and *final.* The first refers to the material substance necessary to establish the effect; the second refers to the plan, theory, and principles to which material substance must comply; the third refers to the effort, or energy, expended to implement the effect; and the fourth refers to the purpose for the sake of which the entire procedure was initiated. For example, in building a house the materials used would constitute the material cause; the blueprint or architect's plans, the formal cause; the energy the workmen exert, the efficient cause; and the purpose of building the house (e.g., to provide shelter), the final cause.

All objects in the world, said Aristotle, are composed of form and matter; the principle of entelechy gives form to matter, thus actualizing (realizing) matter. The world is arranged according to the relative standing each object occupies in the universe, objects of superior form (spirit, or mind) standing relatively higher in the scale. Rocks, minerals, and other inanimate objects, being almost pure matter (unformed matter), are relegated to the lowest end of the scale, while God, incorporeal form, is at the upper end; occupying intermediary positions in ascending order are: vegetation, animal life, and human life. Although the Aristotelian classification of things according to their metaphysical composition of form-matter refers to a type of evolution, it differs from the Darwinian concept in that all things in the Aristotelian system were created at one time; the evolutionary concept used by Aristotle indicates a graduated scale of objects, as contrasted with the gradual process in Darwin's theory with higher forms emerging from lower species.

Finally, Aristotle believed that the cause of all things is a Prime Mover, God, who consists of pure form, free from material composition (for matter is never perfect, since it is in need of perfecting, of actualization). God, the First Mover, himself unmoved, possessing completed actuality, becomes the initial mover, cause, of everything else. Inasmuch as God is pure form, he is also the final cause, the purpose or motivating cause of all things, because it is God who activates the impulse (entelechy) in things to form themselves—to actualize or realize themselves. The Prime

Mover God, incorporeal (immaterial), eternal, immutable, the absolutely independent and perfect Being, is completed actuality; he alone needs no self-realization, for he is fully actualized, hence the highest and best Being or Essence—pure act (actus purus), pure thought.

MODERN POST-CARTESIAN METAPHYSICS

Modern metaphysics stems from the works of the French philosopher René Descartes (1596-1650), a Continental Rationalist. This section will provide a brief over-all view of the metaphysical ideas of nine modern philosophers: the three Continental Rationalists—Descartes, Spinoza, and Leibniz; the three British Empiricists—Locke, Berkeley, and Hume; and the three German Idealists—Kant, Hegel, and Schopenhauer. (For a discussion of contemporary metaphysical thought see the section entitled *Types of Philosophy*.) It should be noted that metaphysical inquiry in the modern period has concentrated on two major areas: the search for an ultimate substance, the ontologically real; the epistemology or methodology—the method of attaining knowledge about the ultimate reality. (Some of the metaphysical problems, a third area, related to the philosophy of religion, have been discussed in the preceding section.)

Metaphysical Dualism of René Descartes. The most influential Metaphysical Dualist of all time, Descartes (1596-1650), postulated that reality consists of two elements: *mind* and *matter*. These two entities exhaust the whole of reality, for what is not mind is matter, what is not matter is mind, and the only other possibility is a combination of both.

Descartes believed the essence of matter to be its characteristic of occupying space (the fact that it is extended, corporeal), whereas the distinctive quality of mind is its spiritual nature, its incorporeality, its nonmaterial nature, the fact that it is not extended, does not occupy space. The nature of the soul is mind, while the nature of physical things is matter. Ultimately, matter is incapable of final proof, whereas mind can be conclusively proved.

Descartes claimed that the reality of soul could be proved with absolute certainty, for the precise reason that it is beyond all doubt. The indubitability of the soul (mind and soul are synonymous for Descartes) arises from the fact that in the very attempt to disprove or doubt the soul, a person finds himself in effect proving it. The proof of the soul is inherent in its disproof, that is, in the attempt to cast doubt upon it, as exemplified in the following dialogue:

"I doubt that I exist."

"But if I do not exist, then who is doing all of this doubting?"

"At least the person doing all of the doubting must exist."

"Since I am doing all of the doubting, then I, the *doubting-doubter*, must exist. I cannot doubt if I do not exist."

The Cartesian statement of this argument is *Cogito, ergo sum* (I doubt, therefore I am).

The fact that man reasons in the above manner, without depending on facts or experience of any sort, convinced Descartes that knowledge exists in the individual at birth, as innate awareness or innate ideas. He concluded further that not only mathematical and logical principles, but also ideas about God and the soul are inborn. Since thinking occurs without requiring experience, the mind or soul which does the thinking must be innate. Similarly the idea of a God must be innate, for it is not dependent upon experience. As for functions of logical reasoning, they are surely innate. For example, the principle of contradiction is innate, for no one will accept a self-contradictory proposition; thus, nothing can be at one and the same time all black and all white, or dead and alive, or present and absent. Human reason insists that only one of these alternative contradictory possibilities can be accepted. Understanding of the principle of contradiction is innate, not required from life experience.

Continental Rationalism. Descartes maintained that truth is derived from reason and consists of a *clear idea*, or logical thought, which proceeds necessarily from one concept to another. Examples are mathematical relationships, such as $2 + 2 = 4$, and syllogistic statements, such as, "If all Bostonians are Americans, and John Doe is a Bostonian, then it necessarily follows that John Doe is an American." Descartes used this method of reasoning in his arguments to prove the existence of the soul, of innate ideas, and of God.

THE PSYCHOPHYSICAL MONISM OF BENEDICT SPINOZA

The Pantheist Spinoza (1632-1677) equated the Being of the universe, its ultimate Substance, with God. He held that God and Substance are one and the same, and that both terms may be used interchangeably; such a view is known as *Metaphysical Monism*. God is infinite, possessing an infinite number of attributes, each attribute of which is infinitely extended with infinite modifications.

Of the infinite number of attributes which God (as Substance) possesses, only two are known: *mind* and *matter*. Since mind and matter are attributes of the same Substance, whatever change occurs in Substance affects both mind and matter. "The order and connection of ideas is the same as the order and connection of things." When mind is affected, a concomitant effect occurs in matter; and when body is affected, a concomitant effect occurs in the soul. Spinoza believed that mind and matter are ultimately two aspects of the same Substance. His theory is called *Psychophysical Parallelism*.

The Spinozistic dictum, *sub specie aeterni* (under the aspect of the eternal) issues from his Pantheism, the belief that all reality is God, and that God is the sum total of all reality. Since reality is God, then reality must be one coherent system; each individual part of reality fits properly (logically) into its respective position. In such a system, the existence of God implies the total absence of evil; evil is relegated to the sphere of ignorance. In fact, said Spinoza, ignorance reflects the failure to conceive of things in their rightful place, under the aspect of the eternal. Moreover, the relative value of objects is determined by their respective position in relation to the eternal. The more important a thing is, the greater its relationship to the eternal. All objects in the world fit logically into position, and all have some definite relationship to God. "The mind's highest good is the knowledge of God, and the mind's highest virtue is to know God." [1] All things have their being in God; all things have a precise logical relationship to God. For thoughts such as these, it is no wonder

---

[1] Benedict Spinoza, *Ethics* (1677), Part IV, Proposition 28.

that the philosopher Novalis called Spinoza a "God-intoxicated philosopher."

THE PANPSYCHISM OF GOTTFRIED WILHELM LEIBNIZ

Leibniz (1644-1716) is known as a *Metaphysical Pluralist* because he asserted that the ultimate substance of the world consists of innumerable atom-like beings, or Monads. These individual substances differ from one another in nature, and each is active, independent of the others, lacking any interaction, for the Monads have "no windows," yet each "mirrors the rest." The Monads function according to the inherent nature which each possesses; consequently when a Monad behaves according to its own foreordained nature, the net result is not real interaction but only the appearance of interaction.

Leibniz attributed this appearance of interaction to a *Preëstablished Harmony,* the design or nature which God ascribed to each Monad. Consider water as an example; hydrogen interacts with oxygen to produce water, but, according to the Leibnizian Doctrine of Preëstablished Harmony, real interaction is lacking, for the hydrogen atoms are not aware of the presence or activity of oxygen atoms, and it is only because each is behaving according to its initial God-given nature that the two in proximity to each other appear to be interacting and to function in harmony to produce water.

In the same way, Leibniz resolved the mind-body problem on the basis of the Doctrine of Preëstablished Harmony: the Monads of mind and the Monads of body, each acting according to their prescribed nature, function in unison to give the outward appearance of interaction.

Leibniz postulated that all reality consists of Monads, and he ascribed to the Monads a mental life, involving a kind of useless activity comparable to the energy ascribed to the atom by modern physicists. For Leibniz, matter was not inert or dead, but energized, activated, and living. In this view, all of reality, the ontologically real, consists of living things. Leibniz must therefore be regarded as an adherent of Panpsychism—the doctrine that all substances possess an inherent psyche or soul.

Leibniz portrayed truth as a dichotomy comprising *truths of reason* and *truths of fact*. Truths of reason are eternal, absolute, and follow necessarily from the principles of logic; such truths are known innately (as Descartes had insisted), whereas truths of fact, being contingent, are derived from experience. The former are understood, apperceived; the latter are merely sensed or perceived. The principles of mathematics and logic are examples of truths of reason, whereas factual data comprise truths of fact, the former being theoretical, the latter experiential. (In addition, there is a special truth in the moral kingdom of God.)

According to Leibniz, truths of fact are determined by the *Principle of Sufficient Reason,* which states that there must be a good and sufficient reason why a particular fact is what it is instead of being some other fact or condition. Thus there must be sufficient reason why friction causes heat, or why fire burns, or why man needs oxygen. There is adequate reason to explain why the entire world and all things in it are what they are instead of being something else. What a chaotic universe this would be in the absence of sufficient reason for all things!

Leibniz was an optimistic philosopher who accepted this world as the best of all possible worlds on the ground that God, who is infinitely good, omniscient, and omnipotent (and therefore knows what the best world is) chose the best world in his infinite goodness, and effected or created the best of all possible worlds by means of his infinite power.

Evils, admittedly present in the world, were necessary during the construction of the existing universe with its important values of morality, intelligence, and freedom. If there were no moral evils in the world, there could be no freedom of choice; if there were no doubts, worries, and problems in the world, there would be no place for human intelligence which deals with such shortcomings. Leibniz pointed out that any world containing the higher values necessarily contains concomitant evils; that the contest between good and evil is inevitable.

In addition to the best of all possible worlds, namely, the existing world, there is for Leibniz another world of which God is Monarch. God's world is the most perfect creation possible; it is a moral kingdom of souls. But these are not animal souls (the latter are only images of the mechanistic universe), and it is only the spirit of man that mirrors God because of man's spiritual qualities. Man enters into a spiritual relationship with God, and thus participates in the moral kingdom. "The assemblage of all minds must make up the City of God, that is to say, the most perfect possible state under the most perfect of monarchs. This City of God, this truly universal monarchy, is a moral world in the natural world, and is the most exalted and the most divine of God's works." [1] God's relationship to the physical world and the moral universe is stated in Leibniz's portrayal of "God as Architect of the machine of the universe and God as Monarch of the divine City of Minds." [2]

THE EMPIRICISM OF JOHN LOCKE

With the possible exception of Francis Bacon and Thomas Hobbes, Locke (1632-1704) did more than all the other great philosophers to establish the empirical movement in British thought. He wrote a number of influential works, among which his masterpiece *An Essay Concerning Human Understanding* (1690) expounds the metaphysical basis for his approach to problems of knowledge and truth.

Empiricism is that system of philosophy which accepts experience instead of logical reasoning *per se* as the source of knowledge. (Etymologically, the term *Empiricism* comes from the Greek *en peira,* meaning in trial or *experiment.*) The British Empiricists maintained that all knowledge or truth is derived from experience, rather than from the logical techniques of the Continental Rationalists.

Locke rejected the Cartesian concept of Innate Ideas and insisted that knowledge is derived only from experience. There is "nothing in the understanding which was not first in the senses." Thus, at birth, the human mind is a blank, a "white paper," or, as philosophers have termed it, a *tabula rasa* (blank tablet).

Commencing with birth, as a person receives sensations, they register upon this tabula rasa mind, as if it were a light sensitive

---

[1] Gottfried Leibniz, *Monadology,* tr. Mary Morris (London: J. M. Dent & Sons Ltd., 1934; original *La Monadologie,* 1714), Nos. 85-86.
[2] *Ibid.,* No. 87.

film exposed through the lens of a camera. The sensations are indelibly imprinted upon the mind. Without sensations, knowledge is impossible. As the mind perceives sensations, it relates or associates them, reflects upon them, a process which Locke regarded as reasoning. Ideas, therefore, are the product of sensations. Personality is the complex accumulation of ideas, and personal identity is gained from the storing of ideas in the memory.

Locke drew a distinction between primary and secondary qualities in the objects of experience. Ideas are in the mind, but qualities are to be found in the physical object itself. The primary qualities of a physical object are constant, inseparable parts of the object itself, such as space, mass, and motion. Its secondary qualities are psychological, sensate, such as color, sound, and taste.

Nevertheless, said Locke, both the primary and the secondary qualities are not really inherent within the real object itself, but are merely its characteristics. Consequently, the question is raised: What is the basic substance which produces these primary and secondary qualities? Is there a metaphysical substance (a thing-in-itself), or do qualities alone exist? For example, is a red rubber ball merely the qualities which comprise it, or does it have an underlying substance? Is the ball merely its spongyness, its redness, its roundness, its softness? Or is there more to it—does it have a metaphysical substance, a reality which produced the qualities?

Locke pleads ignorance; he terms ultimate reality a *Je-ne-sais quoi* (I-know-not-what). Locke reasons:

". . . as I have said, not imagining how these simple ideas can subsist by themselves, we accustom ourselves to suppose some *substratum* wherein they do subsist, and from which they do result; which therefore we call sub*stance*. . . . So that if any one will examine himself concerning his notion of pure substance in general, he will find he has no other idea of it at all, but only a supposition of he knows not what support of such qualities which are capable of producing simple ideas in us; which qualities are commonly called 'accidents.' If any one should be asked . . . 'What is it that solidity and extension inhere in,' he would not be in a much better case than the Indian before mentioned, who, saying that the world was supported by a great elephant, was asked, what the elephant rested on? to which his answer was, 'A great tortoise'; but being again pressed to know what gave support to the broad-backed tortoise, replied—*something, he knew not what.* And thus here, as in all other cases where we use words without having clear and distinct ideas, we talk like children; who, being questioned what such a thing is which they know not, readily give this satisfactory answer, that it is *something;* which in truth signifies no more, when so used, either by children or men, but that they know not what; and that the thing they pretend to know and talk of, is what they have no distinct idea of at all, and so are perfectly ignorant of it, and in the dark. The idea, then, we have, to which we give the general name *substance,* being nothing but the supposed, but unknown, support of those qualities we find existing, which we imagine cannot subsist *sine re substante,* 'without something to support them,' we call that support *substantia;* which, according to the true import of the word, is, in plain English, *standing under,* or *upholding*." [1]

This kind of skeptical denial of substance is known as *Metaphysical Agnosticism,* the belief that ultimate reality is unknowable; Nihilism carries the matter a step further by denying altogether the existence of reality.

THE IDEALISM OF GEORGE BERKELEY

Berkeley (1685-1753), was a great British Empiricist who carried Locke's premises to their ultimate conclusion, namely, that if all knowledge comes from experience, then whatever is incapable of being experienced, cannot exist. "To be is to be experienced" (*esse est percipi*).[2] That which falls beyond the possibility of being experienced is not real.

It was Berkeley's view that the nature of experience (psychological sensations) is mental, spiritual, of the nature of mind, and that consequently all reality must consist of the same kind of spiritual substance or mind. He argued that an analysis of sensations proved that all experience is of a mental nature. Consider,

---

[1] John Locke, *An Essay Concerning Human Understanding* (1690), Bk. II, Ch. 23.

[2] George Berkeley, *A Treatise concerning the Principles of Human Knowledge* (Dublin, 1710; 2nd ed., London, 1734).

for example, the sense of sight: I see a book lying on the desk before me; obviously, my eyes do not leave my body to reach out to the book to retrieve it into my mind, but instead I experience only an image of the book—a psychological or mental image. So the only book I ever really know is an image, a visual image. Similarly, if I touch the book, making physical contact with it, my sense organs of touch do not leave my body or enter into the book to establish sense contact, but remain within my body and merely stimulate a mental sensation. Therefore, the only book I ever experience is a mental one, a spiritual book whose nature or substance is akin to that of mind (not brain).

By means of such arguments Berkeley attempted to prove not only that the entire realm of reality consists of a spiritual substance, but also that non-spiritual *matter* as such does not even exist, for the simple reason that it is not, and cannot be, sensed (experienced). Matter becomes a fiction; even worse, non-mental matter is inconceivable, for whatever is conceived must be thought in the mind; it is impossible for matter to enter the mind—only psychological or spiritual reality can be consciously experienced in the mind. Thus, if matter exists at all, it must have an ideal or mental nature.

The belief of an individual that he alone exists (while the rest of the world exists only in his imagination) is known as Solipsism, or faith in complete subjectivity; it is the belief that the self knows only its own mental states of existence. Berkeley, however, was not an adherent of any such doctrine. (In fact, none of the system-building philosophers have advocated Solipsism.) Berkeley was not a Solipsist, for he believed in objective reality, in the genuine existence of the external world beyond the individual. It was his conviction that God created the universe and also created human souls possessing the power to experience it. But he insisted that the real world consists of an immaterial substance identical in its fundamental nature with experience, ideals, and mind.

Epistemological Dualism is the theory that the *knower* and the *thing known* are two distinct entities. Berkeley is an Epistemological Dualist, a fact which is further proof that he could not possibly have been a Solipsist. In Dualism, the *thing known* is distinguished from the *knower,* whereas to the Solipsist the thing and knower are one, and the world or reality becomes a mere figment of the imagination.

If Berkeley's dictum, "To be is to be experienced" is accepted as true, then what can be said as to the reality of any object which is not experienced? Must it be said that any such object cannot exist? Berkeley's answer is that if God perceives it, it exists; this is another way of saying that anything which could be experienced (even though no person is present to experience it) does exist, but that whatever could never be experienced does not exist.

Since Berkeley portrays all substances as identical with ideas, restricting the metaphysically real universe to the realm of the spiritual or ideal, he is known as a philosophical Idealist.

THE SKEPTICISM OF DAVID HUME

Perhaps the world's greatest systematic Skeptic was another British Empiricist, David Hume (1711-1776), of Scotland. Following in the tradition of Locke and Berkeley, Hume predicated all knowledge on experience. Just as Berkeley had carried Locke's arguments further to arrive at a new interpretation of reality, so Hume made use of Berkeley's ideas as the basis for his novel conclusions.

As an Empiricist, Hume reduced all knowledge to perceptions, from which we obtain impressions and ideas; he then asserted that whatever cannot be perceived by man does not exist. His analysis of those things genuinely perceived indicated to him that much of what previously had been taken for granted should be rejected. The *substance* of the world, the *matter* of which it is composed, cannot be perceived; hence matter does not exist. God is not an object of perceptions, and therefore God cannot be said to exist. Man's soul is not a perception, so the soul does not exist. Laws of science, laws of causation, are not observable either; consequently, science and scientific realities do not exist. Hume's Skepticism is complete, for it states that knowledge of ultimate reality does not exist.

These conclusions led Hume to accept the doctrine of Phenomenalism, which restricts existence to the phenomenal, to that aspect of the world which is perceptual, excluding the world of Ideas or metaphysical reality (the ontologically real). That which is subject to sense observation (any sense perception) exists, while laws of science, the soul, and God cannot be experienced and therefore do not exist.

Hume's Skepticism concerning science is based upon the imperceptibility of natural laws. Consider, for example, the law of gravity. When you observe something fall to earth, you see changes taking place, but you do not sense gravity itself or any law of gravity; in fact, a falling person senses only pressures in the atmosphere, never anything like a principle of gravity. From such reasoning, Hume concluded that laws of science and scientific causation are imperceptible, nonexistent, untrustworthy figments of the imagination.

THE CRITICAL IDEALISM OF IMMANUEL KANT

The breach which existed between the Rationalism of the philosophers on the European Continent and the Empiricists of the British Isles was resolved in a synthesis by the German philosopher Kant (1724-1804) who at first accepted Rationalism and Empiricism individually, but later discovered that neither was acceptable alone. It seemed necessary to synthesize the two divergent philosophies into a compound unit. The principles of German Idealism developed from the Kantian reconciliation of the two philosophical approaches.

To make genuine knowledge possible, both perceptions and conceptions are necessary; sensations provide us with our percept, while the understanding gives us our concept. "Thoughts without content are empty, percepts without concepts are blind. . . . Understanding can perceive nothing, the senses can think nothing. Knowledge arises from their united action" wrote Kant in his most famous work, *The Critique of Pure Reason* (1781, 1787). The two in concert (sensations and understanding) produce genuine knowledge and may be considered analogous to raw material and machinery which work together to produce a finished article. (The raw material may be compared to sensations, the machinery to understanding, and the finished article to knowledge.)

Kant envisioned the world as a three-fold entity: the world of the understanding, man's mind, the world of knowledge—the world as known; the world as sensed, the phenomenal world, the knowable world—the sense-world; and the world of reality, the metaphysical world, the things-in-themselves, the world of ideals, the transcendental world, the noumenal world—the unknowable world.

The first world is in the human being, his mind, and consists of knowledge he derives from the second world, namely, from the world which he senses; but the world he senses needs a base, a primary substance, as Locke had discovered, and this world, a world of substance, produces the sense objects of the phenomenal world. Genuine knowledge, which combines the first world with the second, merely reproduces the third or real world. Human senses cannot penetrate metaphysical reality, but are restricted to sensory phenomena. It is the understanding which utilizes sense data to reconstruct what it logically infers or pictures to be the real world. Reality then, because it cannot be directly apprehended by the senses, is a mental reconstruction, a replica, a miniature working model of what reality must be, judging from the phenomenal world and the mind's rational interpretation of it.

Since the real world, so far as man can possibly rationalize it, is a mental reconstruction, an ideal world of the understanding, then we must conclude the nature of reality to be of the nature of mind, ideal—hence the doctrines known as *Kantian Idealism*.

As noted above, genuine knowledge of the real world is impossible because our senses do not directly register reality; the best they do is to sense phenomena. Reality is transcendental in the sense that it is beyond the reach of the senses. Although phenomena can be sensed, the *thing-in-itself* (the metaphysically real substance) which produces phenomenal objects is permanently beyond the reach of our knowledge; the only knowledge possible to us is the product of a synthesis of sense and understanding, an inference from experience. Sense perception can never transcend the bounds of experience to reach reality; it is a permanent obstacle which prevents us forever from knowing a reality directly. Whatever knowledge we assert regarding reality must therefore be illegitimate, not genuine. This conclusion as to the *inability* of man ever to pierce the bounds of experience and to reach into the transcendental world of reality (and apprehend knowledge of it directly) is known as *Kantian Agnosticism.*

Transcendental objects, the things-in-themselves (or what Kant terms *noumena*), such as God, freedom, immortality, and ideals are illegitimate forms of knowledge since they cannot be sensed but must be accepted on faith. Atheism and Nihilism, too, must be accepted on faith because knowledge of them is also beyond the bounds of experience (transcendental). Transcendental realities, however, do serve mankind as ideas or ideals of reason; they thus give unity to human knowledge and make it a coherent whole when limited sense experience leaves many loose ends and important unanswered questions. The Kantian transcendental world is a supersensible world; since man is restricted to human senses, he must be content with only that limited knowledge of the phenomenal world which can be sensed.

THE ABSOLUTE IDEALISM
OF GEORG WILHELM FRIEDRICH HEGEL

Another German Idealist, Hegel (1770-1831), was greatly influenced by Kant and to some extent by the works of Heraclitus and Spinoza. Hegel is credited with founding the philosophy of religion, the history of philosophy, the philosophy of history, and other philosophical disciplines.

Hegel's permanent contribution to logic (a point of view used by Marx in developing his system of Dialectical Materialism) was a dynamic system of reasoning known as the Hegelian Dialectic, designed to explore the meaning of reality as a process. Dialectic means discourse, a conversation; for Hegel, conversation is the very nature of mind, the manner in which it functions logically. The same Dialectic is the manner in which a progressive nature and a moving reality behave.

The Hegelian Dialectic begins with a *thesis* which by a *principle of negativity* moves to its opposite, called an *antithesis*. The forces of the two in opposition clash, producing an emergent reconciliation of the two which, though new and different, shares aspects of both thesis and antithesis and is called a *synthesis*. For example, the clash of hydrogen (thesis) with oxygen (antithesis) produces water (synthesis); or better still: the clash of Continental Rationalism (thesis) with British Empiricism (antithesis) resulted in German Idealism (synthesis).

The Dialectic theorizes the relatedness of all things, and the Dialectical process interrelates all things. Nothing in the world is isolated; everything is related to, and influenced by, whatever is in its proximity. Ultimately every object is related to every other object in the universe. To explain the meaning of an object is to relate it to other objects, to its antitheses. The more a person is able to establish the relationships of an object, the more he can show how it coheres with other things in the world, the more he has explained it or has proved it to be a fact. Ultimately the whole world is related, each fact to every other; the interrelationship of all facts is called the Coherence Theory of Truth or the Coherence Theory of Reality.

The Coherence Theory of Truth is predicated on the idea that the world is one enormous *rational system,* an Absolute whole. The nature of the Absolute whole, or what Hegel termed the *Idee,* is rational. "The *real is rational* and the rational is real." The rational, when regarded as a systematized whole, the Absolute, is Truth. *"Truth is the whole."*

Because Hegel considered metaphysical reality to be *rational,* a rational system, a coherent absolute whole, the *Idee,* he is known as an Idealist. Kant had asserted metaphysical reality to be unknowable because knowledge is derived from the senses and reality could never be sensed. Hegel, however, claimed that men can and do know reality; they know it because it is a rational system and they are rational beings. Men do not need to sense reality, nor do they in fact sense it; they understand it, reason it out, infer it, figure its nature out logically.

For example, no human being can sense X rays with the unaided sense organs of the body, yet man has gained knowledge of them because these rays possess a very rational nature, behave rationally, and man has been able to reason about them as a means of deriving pertinent information. The rational is real, and the real is rational. "What is this world but the image of REASON. . . ?"

THE PESSIMISTIC VOLUNTARISTIC IDEALISM
OF ARTHUR SCHOPENHAUER

The philosophy of Schopenhauer (1788-1860) is known as *Pessimistic Voluntaristic Idealism;* Pessimistic because he regarded the world as irrational, Voluntaristic because for him the ontologically real substance of the world is *Will* (driving force), Idealism because the metaphysically real substance is of the nature of mind.

The philosophy of Schopenhauer emphasized these concepts: metaphysical reality, the ontologically real, is a blind irrational force, called will, which manifests itself in man as the will to live (drive of self-preservation), but life is essentially a mistake, an evil which man strives to overcome by conquering the will to live.

"The world is my idea," wrote Schopenhauer, and such is the basis of his Idealism. The world which man knows, experiences, feels, understands, senses, is always in the form of an idea. "No truth therefore is more certain, more independent of all others, and less in need of proof than this, that all that exists for knowledge, and therefore this whole world, is only object in relation to subject, perception of a perceiver, in a word, idea." [1] Thus for the subject, the perceiver, the stuff of which the world is made is *idea.*

In actuality, whatever exists must exist solely for the subject, since only the subject possesses experiences; consequently idea and the object of one's idea are identical. "The whole world of objects is and remains idea." Schopenhauerian Idealism is not a dream world, nor Solipsism, an imaginary world, for he distinguishes the real world from dreams, ascribing to the real world continuity of experience and rational cohesion.

In Schopenhauer's view, then, the phenomenal world consists of *idea,* but the ontologically real world consists of *will.* He believed that will is force, the fundamental reality in all objects; that, in man, it is chiefly identified with body instincts of self-preservation and sex, and elsewhere in nature as gravitational

---

[1] Arthur Schopenhauer, *The World as Will and Idea,* tr. R. B. Haldane and J. Kemp (1883). The remainder of the quotations in this section are from the work cited. Original German edition published in Leipzig, 1819.

forces. "Besides will and idea nothing is known to us or think-able." A person's "will is the real inner nature of his phenomenal being, which manifests itself to him as idea. . . . Phenomenal existence is idea and nothing more. All idea, of whatever kind it may be, all *object,* is *phenomenal* existence, but the *will* alone is a *thing in itself.*" The will, as the Kantian thing-in-itself, is not phenomenal but ultimate reality itself, the stuff of which the world is made.

The nature of the ontologically real, the will, is a blind, irrational, indestructible, driving force. Because the will rampages incoherently on its way, without regard for what is intelligent and wise, the philosopher can only be pessimistic about the fate of man and the universe. The will has no regard for individual human life and happiness; consequently, due to the capricious nature of the will, human life regularly encounters misery.

Pain and misery in the world are not accidents, but a positive integral aspect of the nature of reality. Pain and misery are positive, while happiness is negative (in the sense that the period of relief experienced during the cessation or temporary let-up of pain is a state of happiness). For Schopenhauer, "life must be some kind of mistake," and "it is a sin to be born."

Death is no escape from the tyrannous will, for the will is everlasting, and it will prevail in this or any other life; thus, suicide is of no avail. Furthermore, suicide is a cowardly approach, and a clumsy experiment; moreover, if it proved to be a blunder, the individual would have no opportunity to correct it.

Salvation is achieved through annihilation of striving, rejecting desire for life, but not life itself. It is partially attained through art, that is, contemplating the eternal abiding Platonic Ideas, but the fuller form of salvation is the achievement of the greatest good, the highest ideal, *Nirvana,* which requires extinction of all impulses, or at least an attitude of indifference toward them. Thus it is an ideal of *nothingness.*

The highest morality is one of compassion toward our fellow man; since we are all suffering in this present world, it is better not to condemn fellow creatures, but to pity and sympathize with them. This highest morality requires mankind to repress and eliminate all forms of egoistic self-assertion and aggressive competitive striving.

PART SIX—TYPES OF PHILOSOPHY

PART SIX—TYPES OF PHILOSOPHY

There is wide disagreement among philosophers as to which type or school of philosophy is true or, for that matter, best. However, since conflict of ideas is present in all disciplines (including even the sciences), this lack of agreement need not deter us from our quest of the true, the good, and the beautiful, as Plato defined the philosopher's task. Moreover, a conflict of ideas is conducive to the advancement of knowledge. If all men thought alike, their intellectual and material progress would slow down or cease altogether. Fortunately, during the past century, a great diversity of philosophical schools of thought have been widely adopted, such as Dialectical Materialism, Pragmatism, Classical Positivism, Logical Positivism, Neo-Scholasticism, Neo-Thomism, Neorealism, Idealism, Personalism, Phenomenology, and Existentialism.

Before discussing these philosophical schools, we should note that some representative philosophers have changed from one school to another during their lifetime and that quite a few have been able simultaneously to subscribe to separate schools of thought. Thus Bertrand Russell at different stages of his philosophical career adhered to doctrines of Panpsychism, Platonism, Neorealism, Logical Positivism, and Scientism, among others; similarly, another noted philosopher, Moritz Schlick, subscribed both to Logical Positivism in dealing with scientific problems, and to Personalism in dealing with the philosophy of religion. Furthermore, it must be kept in mind that certain contemporary schools of philosophy may enjoy a close kinship because during their development one school may have shared or perhaps somewhat modified the ideas of a preceding school.

DIALECTICAL MATERIALISM

Dialectical Materialism is a philosophy predominantly Communistic, a philosophical school of thought founded originally by Karl Marx; and it survives today owing to wide acceptance in east European and Asian nations whose political structure is Communistic. In recent decades, Soviet Russian Communists have made of it a quasireligion, or *Diamat* (contraction of the term *Dialectical Materialism*). The metaphysical foundation of Dialectical Materialism is antiquated, for its basis is a science over a century old; hence it rests on a rather tenuous foundation. In some respects its view of ultimate reality can be traced back to primitive beginnings among ancient Greek philosophers twenty-five hundred years ago, antedating even the time of Socrates.

In the modern era, Dialectical Materialism has developed along "orthodox" lines set forth by Karl Marx, Friedrich Engels, Nicolai Lenin, and Josef Stalin. The basic Communist position is delineated by Marx and Engels, especially in their classic texts, *Capital* and the *Manifesto of the Communist Party*.

The principal ideas of Marxism are: (1) *Dialectical Materialism*; (2) inherent *class struggle* between laborer and capitalist; (3) *Communism*—the ownership in common of the means of production; (4) *violent revolution*—overthrow of capitalistic governments by force; (5) the *labor theory of value*—the theory that price is determined by man-hours of labor expended on production; (6) *economic determinism*—the decisive influence of economics throughout the history of society; (7) *Dictatorship of the Proletariat*—government by the working class; (8) *atheism*—with religion viewed as the opium of the masses, and religious institutions as a police force devised by capitalistic-dominated religion to deter the masses from overthrowing capitalistic regimes; (9) *withering away of the State*—gradual elimination of the need of established governments; (10) *Historical Materialism*—the theory that material wealth is the source of power; (11) *surplus value*.

The first five of the eleven basic ideas listed above merit further discussion here.

Dialectical Materialism.   Initially, Marx founded his philosophy on the Dialectic of Hegel and the Materialism of Feuerbach, hence the designation *Dialectical Materialism*. In accordance with Hegelian dialectic, he saw the major movements of history clashing and a new era of thought arising as a consequence. Marx asserted that in each era the economic system produces "the germs of its own destruction," a process of dialectical conflict out of which a new period evolves—a process repeated until eventually Communism emerges as the denouement or final stage in the history of civilization.

Inherent Class Struggle (leading to the Dictatorship of the Proletariat). As indicated above, Marx believed that the Dialectic is a driving force bringing two basic movements of history into conflict and that a new movement in history (a movement in the direction of Socialism) emerges from the conflict. In each period of a people's history, the Proletariat (the class of workers) inevitably clash with the Bourgeoisie (the class of employers). Marx assumed that the financial interests of these classes are irreconcilable, and that, since one benefits only at the expense of the other, they can never become allies or partners in a common enterprise. Thus the economic struggle persists until final overthrow of capitalistic power, and establishment of control by the class of workers. As a matter of justice, said Marx, the workers should govern because they, not the capitalists, actually produce the material goods of any society. Permanent control by the workers—the Dictatorship of the Proletariat—is the central goal of Communism.

Communism. The philosophy of Dialectical Materialism, as formulated by Marx, was based upon "the common ownership of the means of production," or, negatively, "the abolition of private property." The basic goal of Communism is the sharing, in common, of those material goods which are the means of production, particularly land and raw materials. In the words of the Communist Manifesto, "the distinguishing feature of Communism is the abolition of bourgeois property." In the modern world, bourgeois private property represents the final stage in economic evolution—a system of production and ownership based on class antagonism, on the exploitation of the many by the few. Consequently, the ideal of the modern Communists may be summed up in the words, "abolition of private property." In the ideal future society, the people as a whole, the community, owns all capital goods, for capital is then a social, not a personal, power.

Violent Revolution. Communists feel justified in resorting to the violent overthrow of existing regimes in order to institute

Proletariat Dictatorships. We may quote again this passage in the Manifesto, which states: "They openly declare that their ends can be attained only by the forcible overthrow of all existing social conditions. Let the ruling classes tremble at a Communistic revolution. The Proletarians have nothing to lose but their chains. They have a world to win. Working men of all countries, unite!" Adherents of democratic philosophies of government, accustomed to processes of peaceful change, regard such an appeal to violence as one of the most reprehensible aspects of Marxism.

The Labor Theory of Value. According to Marx, any object sold on the market should be priced on the basis of the amount of labor (man-hours) expended on production, not on the basis of fluctuating conditions of supply and demand. To repeat our quotation from *Das Kapital*, "That which determines the magnitude of the value of any article is the amount of labor socially necessary, or the labor-time socially necessary for its production. . . . All values, all commodities are only definite masses of congealed labor-time. The value of a commodity would therefore remain constant, if the labor-time required for its production also remained constant." The more time involved in producing any commodity, the greater its value. (As we have already mentioned in Part Three, however, a useless product is devoid of value regardless of the amount of time consumed in its manufacture.)

Thus Dialectical Materialism is predominantly a social or political philosophy. Its greatest weaknesses stem from its metaphysical foundations (based on a concept of matter which antedates contemporary nuclear physical theory) and its advocacy of violent revolution.

PRAGMATISM AND INSTRUMENTALISM

A second type of philosophy, one originating in America and predominantly American, is *Pragmatism*, the philosophy of practical consequences. Most Pragmatists regard metaphysical discussions as inconsequential, hence unimportant, if not meaningless. Since in their view only the practical has any effect on our lives, then only the practical has value; all else is relegated to limbo, there to be kept in a state of suspended judgment.

The royal line of Pragmatists consists of Charles Sanders Peirce, who originated and coined the term Pragmatism; William James, who popularized this school of philosophy by means of comprehensive analyses of its practical foundations; John Dewey, who emphasized the experimental and instrumental aspects of Pragmatism; and F.C.S. Schiller, who linked Pragmatism with Humanism. The salient features of Pragmatism are its (1) criterion of truth, (2) methodology, (3) Instrumentalism, (4) Humanism, (5) Pragmaticism, and (6) theory of truth.

The Pragmatic Criterion of Truth. The workability of an idea is the Pragmatist's criterion of truth; if an idea works, it is true. The truth of an idea is tested by the consequences; an idea void of results is inconsequential, hence meaningless. The Pragmatist ignores ideas which are so completely metaphysical that they contain no practical value. An idea must have, as James puts it, *cash value,* a practical aspect, a useful, consequential element; otherwise, it must be repudiated.

William Ernest Hocking, the eminent idealist philosopher at Harvard University (where both Peirce and James also taught) advocated *Negative Pragmatism,* the theory that what does not work cannot be true. His objection to *Positive Pragmatism* stemmed from the fact that ideas or proposals which appear to be working may eventually be proved to have been false. Within any finite period of time, a theory may seem to work, yet might it not fail utterly at some time during the infinite future? Although an immediate failure disproves an idea, a few successes do not necessarily indicate an enduring truth. The discussion of the criteria of truth (see Part I) pointed out that, in practical experience, as in the treatment of illness, for example, it often happens that use of prescribed medicine precedes a cure even though only a placebo has been administered. Obviously, the patient's faith, not the medication *per se,* was the effective factor. Contrary to Positive Pragmatism, therefore, one can say only that if a theory works, nevertheless, it may or may not be true. If the theory does not work, it cannot be true.

The Pragmatic Theory of Truth. According to Pragmatists, however, truth is the correspondence of an idea with reality—a concrete reality, not an abstract one. Furthermore, there are many truths, not merely one. Ideas become true or are classed as true when they fructify into action. "Truth *happens* to an idea," says James, "it *becomes* true, is *made* true."

Instrumentalism. John Dewey's Pragmatic position was termed Instrumentalism, or, at times, Experimentalism. The Instrumentalist regards ideas or theories as instruments of action, rather than as truths *per se*. Knowledge and ideas are tools, intellectual instruments utilized by the mind for dealing more effectively with practical concrete situations. James explains Dewey's Instrumentalism as follows: Theories are "instruments, not answers to enigmas, in which we can rest. . . . Any idea upon which we can ride, so to speak; any idea that will carry us prosperously from any one part of our experience to any other part, linking things satisfactorily, working securely, simplifying, saving labor, is true for just so much, true in so far forth, true *instrumentally*." Although ideas are only instruments, they are very necessary for successful living.

Humanism. Another interpretation of Pragmatic philosophy, Humanism, was elaborated by the British scholar F.C.S. Schiller, a foremost European Pragmatist. Schiller's Humanism has a kinship with Personalism, for it emphasizes the decisive role of human personality. Truth is a human truth, a fact which comes into existence only by virtue of a human personality. Independent truth, truth extraneous to persons, cannot be—all Pragmatic truth is personal; all consequential truth is related to persons.

Pragmaticism. Pragmatism may be, as James asserted, "a new name for old ways of thinking," but Pragmaticism is Peirce's exclusive label for his own peculiar brand of Pragmatism. When Peirce noted that other philosophers, particularly James, appropriated and used the term *Pragmatism* with a connotation unacceptable to him, he coined a new term *Pragmaticism*, which he was sure would be safe from "kidnappers." Peirce was right, for no one was interested in making use of the term, which, consequently, perished in infancy.

Peirce defined Pragmaticism as follows: "The entire intellectual purport of any symbol consists in the total of all general modes of rational conduct which, conditionally upon all the possible different circumstances and desires, would ensue upon the acceptance of the symbol." [1] In other words, Peirce maintained that the significance of an idea resides in the nature of its consequences. Furthermore, in his view the function of thought is to be found in the production of "habits of action."

A distinction should be drawn between Peirce's Pragmaticism and other forms of Pragmatism: he allows for belief in, and the postulating of, ultimate reality, whereas other Pragmatists shy away from metaphysical discussions.

CLASSICAL POSITIVISM

Auguste Comte, father of sociology, founded the philosophy of Classical Positivism and the religion of Humanism (see discussion of F.C.S. Schiller's view of Humanism, p. 152). For Comte, God, the Great Being, was identical with humanity. Comte's Humanism postulated love as its principle, order as its basis, and progress as its aim; it was a kind of religion without theology, an ethics substituted for dogma. Comte regarded altruism as man's highest duty and blessedness.

According to Comte, human knowledge has undergone three stages of development: (1) the theological stage, (2) the metaphysical stage, and (3) the positive stage.

In the first (the theological) stage, which was the earliest and most primitive, man explains natural phenomena in terms of personal forces, spirits, or gods. Primitive man was polytheistic, ascribing events to the intercession of specified deities (such as the god of thunder, the god of fertility, the goddess of love), each a distinct personality.

In the second (the metaphysical) stage man attributed national phenomena to the working of impersonal forces or principles referred to as scientific laws or laws of nature. Scientific principles replaced the polytheistic gods as controlling forces. Thus the god of gravity was replaced by the law of gravity; the god of power by the laws of horse power; the god of thunder by the laws of sound.

---

[1] *Monist* (1905).

In the third (the Positive) stage, natural phenomena are explained neither in terms of personal spirits nor in terms of impersonal laws or forces. Judgments of fact are based upon careful observation of events verifiable by sense experience. In their attempt to disprove mystic or occult explanations of natural events, the Positivists may go so far as to deny all spiritual realities, such as God, soul, immortality, moral value, truth, beauty, goodness, justice, etc., although some Positivists do not apply their philosophy to value areas but restrict it to the realm of science.

LOGICAL POSITIVISM AND THE ANALYTIC SCHOOL

In 1924, a seminar (known as the Vienna Circle) conducted by Moritz Schlick originated the new philosophy of Logical Positivism. This philosophy was based primarily on the thinking of Hume and Comte, but also owed much of its development to Ludwig Wittgenstein, who laid the foundation for it in his classic *Tractatus Logico-Philosophicus* (1921). In 1936, Alfred Jules Ayer (a Professor at Oxford and a member of the so-called "Cambridge School of Analysis") wrote a lucid book on the essentials of Logical Positivism which has earned itself the status of *the* text in its field.

Variant forms of Logical Positivism include the Analytic School; Logical Atomism; Physicalism; and Scientism. Also related in basic respects to Logical Positivism are the Principle of Verification and Ayer's Emotive Theory of Ethics.

The Analytic School. A great deal of confusion in philosophy may arise from the language employed—vague references, misuse of terms, semantic limitations—a fact which prompted the adherents of the Analytic School to consider the possibility of developing an ideal language free from the defects of existing forms. Such an ideal language must possess the following requisites: (1) it must be capable of resolving philosophical puzzles, (2) it must be constructed formally, and (3) it must be complete in the sense that it provides predicates (words capable of identifying or defining every observable fact as an atomic component of a complex structure).

The Analytic philosophers assumed the task of removing ambiguities from philosophy by careful analysis of the language employed, for an accurate analysis of words used is often an effective means of deciding a philosophical argument. They assert that the significance of language is to be found not in its meaning, but in its use; hence the slogan of this school is: "Don't look for the meaning; look for the use." The members of this philosophical persuasion believe that questions properly formulated will allow, if not produce, clear answers. According to this group, the philosopher's task is essentially remedial, with *linguistic therapy* as his function; for this reason the appellation, *Therapeutic Positivism,* has been applied to this school of thought.

Logical Atomism. Ludwig Wittgenstein and Bertrand Russell (at one time Wittgenstein's teacher) attempted to develop a philosophy based on an ideal language, that is, a language which possesses a *one to one* ratio with facts of observation and which, since it would consist of linguistic atoms comparable to the atoms of physics, would be a type of Logical Atomism. A *one to one* correspondence of language to observable data is envisioned as a language mirror which reflects the structure of the world. Logical Atomism is an attempt with the aid of linguistic analysis to reduce ideas to the lowest logical components possible, thereby imparting illumination to some of the central problems of philosophy.

Physicalism. British Logical Positivists, commonly called *Neo-Positivists,* drifted to Physicalism, a philosophy which regards physics as the only meaningful language; physical bodies alone are verifiable, for they are subject to sense observation. Physicalism is essentially *Materialism,* with roots going back at least to the era of Thomas Hobbes (1588-1679), first of the British Metaphysical Materialists.

Scientism. The system of philosophy known as Scientism is based on the premise that all knowledge is attainable solely by means of the scientific method. Its chief exponent, Bertrand Russell, asserts that "what science cannot discover, mankind cannot know." Scientism precludes all value judgments; it states that, since goodness, beauty, truth, and morality cannot be proved, they cannot be said to exist. Values are reduced to emotions and consequently are unverifiable. The critic of Scientism may well ask crucial questions about its moral implications: e.g., how could the brutalities of a Nero or a Hitler be proved immoral?

The Principle of Verification. Adherents of this principle point out that statements and judgments can be accepted as meaningful and valid only to the extent that they are verifiable by means of sense experience. Apart from the prescribed realm of sensory experience, assertions and propositions remain meaningless, invalid. Consequently, this school of philosophy regards all metaphysical or mystical things (e.g., God, soul, morals, goodness, beauty, ultimate reality) as unverifiable, hence illegitimate, objects of knowledge. To these philosophers, only statements of fact are meaningful, for they alone can be subjected to verification by means of sense perception. Sensory experience renders statements meaningful and verifies their factual content.

Those who accept the Principle of Verification involve themselves in a logical dilemma, for this principle must itself be rejected as invalid since it is not subject to sensory verification.

The Emotive Theory of Ethics. Alfred Jules Ayer, the Logical Positivist, developed a Neo-Positivist interpretation of ethics based on the view that moral values are neither objective nor subjective, but emotive. Inasmuch as the Principle of Verification depends upon sensory experience, which cannot be applied to moral principles, these Logical Positivists deny the validity of ethical values. They assert that right and wrong behavior is not a reality to be evaluated (for, in fact, value judgments do not exist) but is merely a mode of self-expression. Ayer does not regard moral actions as evidence of the individual's feelings, as Ethical Subjectivists claim, but rather as events wholly outside the domain of valid knowledge. According to the Emotive Theory, to express abhorrence in the presence of murder is not to evaluate it as an objective fact, but to emote, to give expression to feelings: thus, the statement that murder is immoral is equivalent to asserting that it disturbs one emotionally, without in any way ascribing to the act any objective moral quality.

NEO-SCHOLASTICISM AND NEO-THOMISM

Neo-Scholasticism, a philosophy encompassing various systems of thought, such as Neo-Thomism, Scotism, Saurezianism, and Augustinianism, has attracted a great many Roman Catholic adherents. (Note that although some of these Neo-Scholastics may be regarded as Realists, or more accurately as Moderate Realists in metaphysics, they should be carefully distinguished from non-Scholastic Realists, such as Neorealists or Critical Realists.) In this discussion, we shall review some main tenets of Scholastic and Thomistic philosophies.

Scholasticism. The Scholastic philosophy of the Schoolmen during medieval times centered in European universities and became dominant on the Continent both as a method of inquiry and as a philosophy. (1) The Scholastic method was developed as a means of arriving at preconceived conclusions of the Church; and philosophical theories deviating from the established beliefs of the Church were denounced. (2) Scholastic philosophy was dominated by the ideas of Saint Thomas Aquinas (1225-1274), whose point of view was mainly Aristotelian.

Neo-Thomism. Saint Thomas' philosophy, modified in certain particulars by later philosophers—e.g., Descartes, Kant, Heidegger—is the basis for the philosophical system known as Neo-Thomism whose principal champions are Jacques Maritain and Étienne Gilson. (It should be noted that, in 1879, in his encyclical *Aeterni Patris,* Pope Leo XIII declared Thomism to be the official philosophy of the Roman Catholic Church. Some Roman Catholic philosophers have interpreted the encyclical to mean that Thomistic philosophy is acceptable but is not necessarily the only philosophy acceptable to Roman Catholics.)

Scholastic Method of Inquiry. Scholastic philosophers state that faith and reason, each a distinct and equally reliable method of attaining truth, do not conflict, ideally and ultimately, but that faith is the superior of the two owing to its ability to derive truth with both certainty and alacrity, and, furthermore, has the added advantage of being able to discern truths which apparently lie beyond the scope of reason. On the other hand, reason is one indispensable source, for many truths are acquired solely through reason—for example, the fact that water consists of H_2O is not revealed by Sacred Scriptures nor is it dependent upon the authority of the Church. Moreover, although truth issues from either royal road, faith or reason, some truths (e.g., the fact that God exists) are derived from both sources (rational philosophy and revealed religion) as contrasted with truths (e.g., the fact that the Trinity is real) derived solely from faith.

According to the Scholastic philosophers, then, the dual paths

to truth and their reciprocal relationships to each other may be
illustrated in the following diagram:

- - - - - - - - - - - THE ENTIRE RANGE OF TRUTH - - - - - - - - - - -
                    (as known to omniscient God)
       - - - - - - a. Truths derived through reason - - - - - -
             - - - - - - b. Truths derived through faith - - - - - -
       - - c. Truths obtained through either or both sources - -

The Philosophy of Being. Thomism is a philosophy of Realism, for it affirms the ultimate existence of substance; it states
that there are three different basic things, or kinds of Being: (1)
actual Being, (2) potential Being, and (3) God's Being. Thomists hold that an object, if it truly exists, must exist as a metaphysical Being, not merely as essence (the latter being merely a
mental representation of the external object). Essences, as ab-
stractions which the mind has derived from metaphysical Being,
are theoretical in nature, not real in the sense of possessing a
Being of their own. The value of essence lies in the necessity of
the mind to utilize them for purposes of understanding, explaining, theorizing. Essences provide the intellect with conceptions
of reality necessary for understanding reality.

Actual Being. Ultimate reality is not limited to mere essences,
or *quiddities,* as they are often termed, but consists of *Existents*
—each of which truly exists as a Being in its own right. *Truth*
consists in the detection of these *Existents,* and is defined as the
"adequation of intellect and thing." Truth is composed of both
intellect and its corresponding Existent; thus, truth does not
rest merely within the intellect, but lies conjoined in things as
well.

Potential Being. Within Thomistic metaphysic are to be
found the concepts of *act* and *potency,* with the former enjoying
primacy over the latter. Being, that is, *to be,* is to act; in this
respect, Thomism is an Existential philosophy. Potency, or
potentiality, as it is sometimes called, is merely an aspect of
Being; a process of self-realization (or actualization) transforms
potential into actual Being.

A potential object is not real until it is realized, not actual until
actualized; an individual self, for example, is not a person until
he achieves self-realization or self-actualization.

God's Being. In contrast to other forms of Being, God, wanting nothing, completely realized, is alone *Actus Purus,* free from all potential, need, want, hence perfect. God, as pure form or spirit, is immaterial, whereas potentiality is characteristic of materiality.

Thomistic Theory of Evolution. Although Saint Thomas offers a theory of evolution, it is unlike the Darwinian form in several major respects, for Thomas conceives of God as creating the world in one fell swoop at a given time in the past, not as a gradual, intermittent, state of creation; he does not accept the idea that lower forms produced the higher, but states that lower species were created for the sake of the higher species, man.

The Thomistic theory of evolution portrays the evolutionary process as a series of gradations in Being from lower to higher forms of existence. Brute matter exists at the lowest end of the scale, potential matter is higher on the scale, and pure form, God, is at the highest point. Along the ascending scale between the lowest and highest ranks are to be found potential matter (such as minerals and vegetation), animal life, human beings, and angels.

Moderate Realism. The Thomists believe that all Existents from the level of man down to the lowest form of matter consist of both matter and form; for this reason Thomism is designated as a Moderate Realism, that is, as a combination of Idealism and Materialism.

Thomistic Social Philosophy. The political philosophy of Saint Thomas is based upon his metaphysics. Since objects are found in varying degrees along the evolutionary scale of existence, it logically follows that a political society should be ordered accordingly; that is to say, nature, by countenancing inequalities, is aristocratic, not democratic, and hence the proper State should be one in which superior persons govern the inferior.

An ideal State is one with a monarch at its head, assisted by aristocrats forming the upper echelons of government, with democracy practiced only on the lower or grass roots level of society. Saint Thomas explains it thus: "The best form of government is in a state or kingdom, wherein one is given the power to preside over all, while, under him, are others having governing powers. And yet a government of this kind is shared by all, both because all are eligible to govern and because the rulers are chosen by all. For this is the best form of polity being partly kingdom, since there is one at the head of all; partly aristocracy, in so far as a number of persons are in authority; partly democracy —i.e., government by the people—in so far as the rulers can be chosen from the people, and the people have the right to choose their rulers." [1]

NEOREALISM AND CRITICAL REALISM

Neorealism and Critical Realism are philosophical systems developed mainly by twentieth-century American philosophers. The founders of Neorealism in the United States included Ralph Barton Perry, Walter T. Marvin, Edwin G. Spaulding, Edwin B. Holt, Walter B. Pitkin, and William Pepperell Montague, all of whom refused to accept contemporary philosophies of Idealism and Materialism and sought to establish a philosophical school of their own. The founders of Critical Realism included Durant Drake, Arthur O. Lovejoy, James Bissett Pratt, Arthur Kenyon Rogers, George Santayana, Roy Wood Sellars, and Charles Augustus Strong. (Sellars eventually founded his own divergent school of Physical Realism, a form of Materialism.)

Neorealism. Basic principles of Neorealism are as follows:

1. Separation of Metaphysics from Epistemology. Ultimate reality does not depend upon the human being's cognitive processes for its existence, since it can and does exist apart from it. Idealistic philosophers, such as Berkeley, contended that reality is nonexistent apart from the knower, the human being; consequently, the existence of objects of reality depends upon the experience of the knower. The Realist repudiates this claim of Berkeleyan Idealists, asserting reality to be independent of the knowing process.

2. Naive Realism. In order to support their position that reality exists apart from the cognitive process, Neorealists resort to Naive Realism, which considers objects of reality to be precisely as our

---

[1] Saint Thomas Aquinas, *Summa Theologica,* tr. Anton C. Pegis (New York: Random House, 1945), I-II, Q. 105, Art. 1.

senses depict them. Things are as they appear to the senses. Not only does the table before me appear as a table with a top and four legs, but its ultimate nature, or reality, is exactly as my senses record it.

3. Epistemological Monism. Naive Realists are Epistemological Monists, holding to the belief that I, the knower, and the object of my knowledge (e.g., the table) are one and the same. My senses reflect the table; they mirror the table, but are not distinct from the table cognitively. My knowledge of the table and the table itself are involved in a single process and each element is indistinguishable from the other.

4. The Repudiation of Subjectivism. The foregoing discussion implies that Subjectivism (the belief that objects are merely constructs within the organism sensing them) is erroneous. In other words, objects exist independently of the person to whom they are known; furthermore, since a person's knowledge constitutes an inseparable part of the external objects known to him, knowledge *per se* is as objectively real as the objects themselves. Accordingly, knowledge is never mere opinion (subjective); it is an objectively real part of the object known, hence much more than a mental construct.

5. Metaphysical Pluralism. The belief that ultimate reality is composed, not of one kind of substance, but of many different entities, independent of each other, is termed Metaphysical Pluralism, one of the tenets of Neorealism. Metaphysical Pluralism follows logically from the Neorealist's premises. Since objects present themselves to the senses as distinct and mutually independent of each other (as Naive Realism indicates), they must be so ultimately (in reality). Thus, reality is comprised of many different entities.

6. Platonic Realism. Neorealists believe in the ultimate and objective existence of things around them as possessing ontological reality, that is, reality in and of itself alone. It is true that Neorealists differ as to the nature of the ontologically real, but they agree on its genuine existence and refer to it as an independent being resembling the *Idea* of Plato. Real things are therefore comparable in nature to principles, such as are laid down in mathematics or logic.

7. Neutral Entities. The Neorealist Ralph Barton Perry, seeking to avoid a choice between the two conflicting views on ontologically real objects (either as material or as mental), posited the existence of *neutral entities*; these constitute neither a spiritual nor a material but rather a *tertium quid,* a third or neutral reality which sometimes appears to be material, at other times mental. This doctrine is referred to as *neutral monism.*

8. The Method of Analysis. Neorealists believe that the nature of the ontologically real as a neutral entity was derived by analysis. Reducing an object of sense to its smallest part discloses it to be neither mind nor matter, but a neutral substance.

Analysis is also the Neorealist's criterion of truth or method of explanation. To prove or to explain any object successfully is to analyze it, reduce it to its smallest component part. The explanation of an object is not found in its purpose, a teleological explanation, but in its analysis, its ultimate reduction to each atomic part of which an object is composed.

9. The Ego-Centric Predicament. Perry coined this term to signify the completely mental situation of the human being in his knowledge of the external world. Every aspect of man, related to his knowing the objects which surround him, is reduced to the nature of mind. Man's sensations, knowledge, reason, thoughts, ideas, concepts, feelings, and experiences are mental. Whatever fact comes to man from the outside world must be converted into mental qualities before it can enter his mind. Consequently, even if the world of reality happens to be nonmental, it must first be transformed into a mental nature for the mind of man to grasp or entertain it. Human knowledge is mental, whether it be in the form of experience, or in the form of an idea, or in the form of sensation, or in any other form. The Idealist would contend that since the ego-centric predicament is true, then reality cannot be material, but must be a substance of the nature of mind.

Critical Realism. Critical Realists were in accord with Neorealists on most tenets, but differed sharply in their adherence to Epistemological Dualism, the belief that the knower and the object of his knowledge are two distinct and separate entities. Epistemological Monism, a cardinal tenet of Neorealism, was incapable of explaining past events of history. Monism assumes that both knower and the object known are identical; yet, if this is the case, how is it possible to know past events? Consequently, dualism of knower and known is necessary for the adequate explanation of cognition.

PERSONALISM

Three contemporary philosophies are predominantly of American origin: Pragmatism, Neorealism, and Personalism. We have discussed the main features of Pragmatism and Neorealism. Personalism, which considers personality to be the key to reality, may be defined as a philosophy which regards only persons as ultimate and of infinite intrinsic value; outside of personality there is neither value nor reality. The universe itself must be understood in personal terms, as of the nature of personality. Minds alone exist, both individual minds and a Cosmic Mind, God. Although Personalists may also be atheistic, most of them believe in a personal God.

Among the foremost American adherents of Personalism are the founders, Borden Parker Bowne and George H. Howison; and the most active proponents, Albert Cornelius Knudson, Edgar Sheffield Brightman, and Ralph Tyler Flewelling. The European philosopher Charles Bernard Renouvier belongs to this school of philosophy. Two major centers of Personalism in the United States are Boston University and the University of Southern California, at the latter of which the influential journal *The Personalist* is published.

There are nine major tenets of the philosophy of Personalism, as listed below.

1. Personality as the Key to Reality. Personalists maintain that "the key to reality is personality." Ultimate reality is of the nature of personality; the human individual is both an ultimately real entity and personal, as are the other realities—the universe, the activity of God, the Cosmic Mind. Outside of personality, nothing can be intelligently explained or understood. Meaning is significant only for persons; value has worth only for persons; existence has meaning only for persons; beauty is aesthetic only for persons;

morality has meaning only for persons. God, too, has meaning only in the light of personality, as do ideals, purpose, and the whole gamut of the world's significant and valuable objects.

2. *Values as Existing in and for Persons Solely*. Outside of personality there are no values, for these exist exclusively in and for persons. It is because persons are evaluators that they impute value to objects. Value is meaningless extraneous to persons. If persons did not exist in the world, neither would value because only persons ascribe value to nonpersonal things. Before human beings appeared on earth, however, objects possessed value because God, the Supreme Person, invested them with value.

To clarify their point of view, Personalists ask us to put ourselves in the place of God himself, engaged in creating two worlds: the first ugly, evil, and vile; the second beautiful, good, and praiseworthy. Would there be any real difference between two such worlds if there were no place for human beings in them? Since God, the Supreme Person, would be completely independent of and separate from both worlds, there could be no basis for choice between the two. Only rational human beings as reservoirs of value actually impart value to things.

3. *Persons as of Infinite Intrinsic Value*. Individuals possess dignity, infinite intrinsic value, and ultimate worth. Nonpersonal objects have either instrumental value or intrinsic value, but they do not possess *infinite* intrinsic value. Objects other than persons have exchange value, a price for which they can or may be exchanged, but persons are above all price. If there were such a thing as a value scale with a single person on one side, nothing, not even all the treasures of the world, could balance the scale on the other side, except another person or persons. Since each person is of infinite worth, a thousand persons placed on the other side of the scale would merely balance it; infinity multiplied a thousand times equals infinity. Nothing in the world is of sufficient value to be exchanged for a person.

4. *The Universe as Friendly to Values*. The assumptions that the World-Ground is a Cosmic Mind, a Supreme Person, and that values exist in and for persons alone mean that the world is friendly to values. Moreover, since the world is friendly to values,

a Supreme Person must exist; one assumption implies the other. Progress toward fulfillment of values is possible only on the premises that values exist and that the universe functions in accord with them. A life endowed with value operates in harmony with the world; fundamental reality negates a valueless or evil world.

5. *The Individuality of Reality.* Personalists agree with Neorealists that the world is ultimately composed of individual entities. Only the individuals exist, whether they be individual persons or individual things; universals or generalizations do not exist. Thus, there is no such thing as a universal humanity, for only individual human beings exist.

6. *Reality as Activity.* The ultimately real is not a dead inert substance, but a dynamic, active substance, as the energized activity of the atom testifies. The world is God's activity.

7. *The Phenomenality of Matter.* Matter is not an ultimate substance, ontologically real, but is phenomenal only, an apparent object merely, a manifestation of the real. Matter is the data of sense, not the reality which underlies sense objects; matter is a characteristic which reality assumes, but it is not ultimate nor real in the sense of possessing ontological existence.

8. *Volitional Causality.* Personalists believe in the reality of causation. Causes are not mere principles residing in the mind of man, but real active forces that exist in the outside world and are independent of man's thoughts and wishes.

9. *The Unity of the World and World-Ground.* Although the world is composed of different objects, they are nevertheless united by a World-Ground, a Cosmic Person (God). Personality is the only entity capable of uniting diversity in unity, for a person is a *unitas multiplex* (William Stern's term designating a multiple unity), many yet one, change yet permanence and identity.

PHENOMENOLOGY AND PHENOMENALISM

One of the more recent schools of philosophy, Phenomenology, was sired by the German philosopher, Edmund Husserl (1859-1938); also, the contemporary philosophy of Existentialism may be regarded as an outgrowth of his point of view. Phenomenology must be distinguished from Phenomenalism: the latter states that nothing except our sense experiences exists.

Phenomenalism. As noted above, David Hume, the British Empiricist, departing radically from the Empiricists who antedated him, denied the existence of ultimate reality. Hume's Empiricism (based on the assumption that knowledge is derived exclusively from experience—from the impressions which our senses make upon us) concludes that only sense data (phenomena) can be known, and that the objects (ultimate realities) of sense manifestations can never be known. Accordingly, phenomena are the only kind of reality that is verifiable; in fact, metaphysical reality cannot be accepted as a valid assumption.

To illustrate: the sound I actually hear (phenomenal sound) exists, but the sound waves ordinarily assumed to be the real sound do not even exist; the stone I see falling is real, but the law of gravity (which I do not sense) is not a fact of experience. It may be argued that the law of gravity is ultimately real, hence transcends sense detection; but Hume would contend that, since gravity is beyond sense verification, it is devoid of any existence. For Hume, sensing is believing; what is not sensed is nonsense.

Phenomenology. Phenomenology, differing markedly from Phenomenalism, asserts that realities other than mere appearance (phenomena) must be conceded, that objectively real things exist. Husserl refers to these metaphysically real things as essences. An essence is an ideally real structure of phenomena, intellectual in nature. Man's cognitive processes derive essences from the phenomenal experiences presented to his consciousness; by attending and grasping whatever flows through his consciousness, without allowing preconceived biases to interfere or prejudice his empirical findings, man abstracts reality from a multiplicity of phenomenal experiences.

Phenomenologists believe further that essences are derived from the total gamut of human experiences—not merely from the phenomena representing physical things, but also from religious experiences and value judgments. Consider, for example, the familiar psychological effects of injustice. Even the youngest child feels injustice keenly; thus, if two children are punished unequally for the same misbehavior, the child enduring the more severe penalty senses the inherent injustice to which he is being subjected. This awareness of injustice is a genuine experience, the essence of which can be abstracted for analysis and understanding by a process designated by Husserl as *bracketing* or *phenomenological reduction.*

Although Husserl founded Phenomenology, it remained for another German philosopher, Max Scheler (1874-1928), to apply it cogently to the area of values. These philosophers built their philosophical edifice on the foundations laid by the Phenomenalism of David Hume; the Cartesian system resting on Descartes' assertion, "I think, therefore I exist."; Platonic Idealism; and Kant's transcendentalism. Phenomenology may be regarded as basically a form of Neo-Idealism.

EXISTENTIALISM AND NEO-ORTHODOXY

Two main schools of Existentialist philosophy may be distinguished; the first is religious as delineated by the father of Existentialism, Søren Aabye Kierkegaard (1813-1855); the second is atheistic, as expounded by its most articulate contemporary spokesman, Jean-Paul Sartre. A number of outstanding Existentialists in each of these schools disclaim the Existentialist label; some adherents of the religious view prefer to be known as Neo-Orthodox philosophers.

Existentialism Defined. Existentialists accept the conclusion that "existence precedes essence," and some go even further and affirm that essence does not exist, that only existence has reality. All Existentialists emphasize the person as subject. The subject exists, and for some, he alone exists; that is to say, if any essence whatever exists, it is the individual's subjective state of existence.

The Human Being and His Freedom of Will. Although all Existentialists lay great stress upon man's innate freedom, which holds man responsible for all his actions—for the development or outcome of his personality—some, including Sartre, believe that man is born devoid of any characteristics of so-called "human nature." According to Sartre man is not born with any given nature but develops one as he goes through life making decisions. If man has any nature whatever, it is what he *has* been, the personality trail which he leaves behind as he chooses confronting courses of behavior. We make our nature, we do not have one ready-made, and hence we are responsible for the nature we presently possess. Man is constantly in the making; he creates himself by the choices he makes. Therefore man, in existing, chooses his essence (human nature).

As a result of the enormous pressures of responsibility weighing heavily upon a person, and the pressure of choices with their grave accompanying consequences, man experiences a sense of anxiety, for it is a dreadful thought for him to come to the conscious realization that his choices are actually shaping reality. Religious Existentialists, aware of this ominous impending dread and the fact that human reason is impotent and unreliable, turn to God, seeking guidance through revelation. Nevertheless, man is always held responsible for his actions, nor can he escape responsibility by refusing to act at all, for he is always caught in *engagement* with life, always in *involvement with* momentous decisions.

The Philosophy of Irrationalism.   Existentialists do not believe in a rationally ordered reality, but in a subjective, irrational human existence, whose decisions, choices, and behavior are executed independently of reason. Subjective man is motivated by feeling, anxiety, irrational impulses, which override whatever decision his rational forces can rally. Existence is not rational, but permeated with intense feeling, anxiety, forlornness, abandonment, despair, which become man's criteria for knowing truth.

The mind of man is incapable of discovering truth through reason, since truth is found only in paradox. From the vantage point of God, truth is clearly seen as rational, but from the midst of subjectivity in which man finds himself, truth appears contradictory, a paradox.

Subjectivity as Both Truth and Reality.   Kierkegaard wrote, "Subjectivity is truth, subjectivity is reality." [1] From what has been said earlier, this conclusion inevitably follows. Truth is not

---

[1] Søren Kierkegaard, *Concluding Unscientific Postscript*, tr. David F. Swenson, Lillian Marvin Swenson, and Walter Lowrie (Princeton: Princeton University Press, 1941); original published in 1846.

around us, it is in us; however, this statement is not to be construed as meaning that truth is subjective in the sense that it is merely a matter of opinion. Genuine reality is not external to us; it is in us. Generalizations or laws of human nature are not true, but we, as existing human individuals, are real. Thought is not true reality, but the act of thinking is; a decision is not true reality, but deciding is; man described as a human being is not a reality, but he exists as an individual person. Truth is inner, as is reality, for the world of the Existentialist consists of inner subjectivity.

INDEX

Accident, fallacy of, 18-9
Adaptation argument, 94-5
Ad baculum argument, 17-8
Ad hominem argument, 18
Ad ignorantiam argument, 16
Ad misericordiam argument, 16
Ad populum argument, 18
Ad verecundiam argument, 17
Agnostic realism, 91
Agnosticism, 100, 135
  Kantian, 140
Alexander, Samuel, 92
Ambiguity, fallacy of, 12-3
Amoral, 31-2
Amphibology, fallacy of, 13-4
Analogy, argument for immortality, 113
Analogy, false, 22
Analytic method, 162
Analytic philosophy, 154-6
Anaxagoras, 123
Anaximander, 121
Anaximenes, 121
Andronicus of Rhodes, 119
Animism, 92
Anselm, Saint, 95-7
Anthropological argument, 99-100
Anthropomorphic fallacy, 22
Anthropomorphism, 102-3
Antithesis, 140
Apeiron, 121
Appeal to force argument, 17-8
Appeal to ignorance argument, 16
Appeal to pity argument, 16-7

Aquinas, Saint Thomas, 24, 157
  doctrine of soul, 105
  legal philosophy, 65-8
Arguing in a circle, 20-1
Argument from adaptation, 94-5
Argument from analogy, 112
Argument from design, 94
Argument from fear, 101-2
Argument from values, 97-8, 111-2
  for God, 97-8
  for immortality, 111-2
Arguments for atheism, 100-4
  Anthropomorphic, 102-3
  chaotic universe, 100-1
  Evolutionary, 102
  fear, 101-2
  Naive Realism, 103-4
  Who made God? 103
Arguments for existence of God, 92-100
  Anthropological Argument, 99-100
  argument from adaptation, 94-5
  argument from design, 94
  argument from values, 97-8
  Axiological Argument, 97-8
  Epistemological Argument, 99, 101
  Etiological, 92-3
  first cause, 92-3
  Moral Argument, 97, 112
  Ontological Argument, 95-6
  Religio-Empirical Argument, 98-9
  Teleological, 93-4

171

Arguments for immortality, 108-13
  analogy, 112
  conservation of values, 111-2
  Moral, 112
  transmission theory, 113
  universality of belief, 113
Aristippus, 37
Aristocracy, Aristotelian, 63 ff.
  Platonic, 61-2
  Rousseau, 75
Aristotle, 14, 24, 106
  ethics, 33-7
  metaphysics, 119, 126-8
  political philosophy, 62-5
Artisans, 61
Aryan race, 50
Atheism, 100-4, 140, 148
  arguments for, 100-4
Atomism, Logical, 155
Atomists, 123-5
Augustinianism, 156
Authority, as criterion, 8-9
  fallacy of misplaced, 21-2, 112
Autonomy of will, 46-7
Axiogenesis, 92, 111
Axiological argument, 97-8, 111-2
Axiosoteria, 92, 111
Ayer, Alfred Jules, 154 ff.

Bacon, Francis, 133
Becoming, 123
Begging the question, 20-1
Behaviorism, 104-5, 110
Being, 121 ff.
  actual, 158
  God's, 159
  philosophy of, 158, 166-7
  potential, 158
Bentham, 41-3
  dictum, 44-5
  four sanctions, 42-3
  Hedonistic calculus, 42
  summum bonum, 42
Bergson, Henri, 95
Berkeley, George, 107, 128, 135-7

Blanshard, Brand, 25
Bourgeoisie, 79, 149
Bowne, Borden Parker, 88, 102, 105, 163
Bradley, Francis Herbert, 25, 119
Brightman, Edgar Sheffield, 25, 92, 112, 115, 163
British empiricists, 133-8, 141
Browning, Robert, 113
Buddha, 98
Butler, Joseph, 112

Carnap, Rudolf, 25
Categorical Imperative, 45-6
Cause, efficient, 127
  final, 127
  formal, 127
  material, 127
  volitional, 165
Circle in the proof fallacy, 20-1
Circular reasoning, 20-1
City of God, 133
Civil disobedience, 65
Civil law, 67-8, 71-2, 75
Class, Marx, 79-80
  Plato, 60-2
Class struggle, 79, 148, 149
Classical Positivism, 153-4
Coherence, criterion of truth, 10-1
  theory of reality, 141
  theory of truth, 25, 141
Commonwealth, Hobbes, 72
Communism, defined, 78, 149
  Marxian, 78-81, 147-50
  Platonic, 61
Composition fallacy, 14-5
Composure, 38 ff.
Compound questions, 20, 103
Comte, 90, 153-4
Conceptions of God, 87-92
Conceptions of truth, 24-7
Connaturality, 66
Consensus gentium, 7
Conservation of energy, 124
Consistency, loose, 10
  rigorous, 10

Constitution, Hegelian, 76

Constitutional monarchy, 76-7

Continental Rationalists, 128-33, 141

Contract, social of Hobbes, 69-72 Rousseau, 73-5

Contradictory premises, 23

Contrary to fact conditional error, 22-3

Converse fallacy of accident, 19

Correspondence, 8, 24

Cosmological Argument, 93

Cosmology, 32, 93, 120, 121

Courage, 60

Criteria of truth, 3-11
authority, 8-9
coherence, 10-11
consensus gentium, 7
consistency, 10
correspondence, 8
custom, 4
defined, 3
emotion, 5
feelings, 5
hunch, 6
instinct, 5-6
intuition, 6
majority rule, 7
naive realism, 7-8
pragmatic, 9
revelation, 6-7
rigorous consistency, 10
time, 4-5
tradition, 4

Criterion of morality, Aristotle, 36-7
Kant, 45-6
Mill, 43-4
Moore, 53-4

Critical Realism, 160, 162-3

Custom, 3, 4

Cyrenaic Hedonists, 37

Darwin, Charles, 94, 100

Darwinian theory, 94-5

Death, 38

Deism, 89-90

Deistic Supernaturalism, 90

Democracy, 63-4, 75

Democritus, 63-4, 75, 124, 125, 126

Deontological ethic, 45-8

Descartes, 96-7, 106, 120, 157, 167
metaphysics, 128-9

Design argument, 94

Determinism, economic, 80, 148

Dewey, John, 91, 151, 152

Dialectic, 77, 122, 140-1

Dialectical Materialism, 78-81, 140, 147-50

Diamat, 140

Dictatorship, Machiavelli, 68-9
Marx, 79, 148

Dicto simpliciter fallacy, 18-9

Dignity of man, 47

Divine arbitrariness, 107

Division fallacy, 15

Dualism, mind-body, 106

Dysteleology, 114-5

Economic determinism, 80

Education, Platonic, 61

Ego-centric predicament, 162

Egoism, 37

Elan Vital, 95

Eleatic philosophy, 121-3

Emergent Evolution, 95

Emotion, 5

Emotive language fallacy, 12

Emotive theory of ethics, 156

Empedocles, 123

Empiricism, 133-8
defined, 133

Engels, Friedrich, 148

Entelechy, 127-8

Entities, neutral, 162

Epictetus, 38, 40, 41

Epicureanism, 37-8

Epicurus, 37-8

Epiphenomenalism, 104-5

Epistemological Argument, 99, 101
Epistemological Dualism, 136-7, 162-3
Epistemological Monism, 161, 162-3
Epistemology, 1-28, 120
  defined, 3
Equality, Rousseau, 73
Equivocation, 13
Eternal law, 67
Ethical Intuitionism, 45-8
Ethical realism, 53
Ethics, 31-55
  Bentham, 41-3
  Cyrenaic, 37
  defined, 31
  Epicurean, 37-8
  Kantian, 45-8
  Mill, John Stuart, 43-5
  Moore, George E., 53-5
  Naturalism, 50-2
  Nietzschean, 50-2
  Realism, 53-5
  Royce, 52-3
  Schopenhauer, 48-50
  scope, 31
  Self-Realization, 33-7
  social, 32
  Socratic, 32-3
  Stoicism, 38-41
Etiological Argument, 92-3
Evil, escape from, 49
  as parasitic, 47
  problem of, 113-5
Evolution theory, Bergson, 95
  Darwin, 94-5
  Morgan, 95
  Thomistic, 159
Evolutionary Argument, 102
Existentialism, 23, 26, 158, 165, 167-9
  defined, 167
Experimentalism, 152

Fallacies of reasoning, 11-23
  irrelevant evidence, 12, 16-8
  linguistic, 12-6

False analogy, 22
False cause fallacy, 19
Feelings, 5
Feuerbach, 90, 148
Figure of speech fallacy, 14
Finite series, 111
First cause, 92-3
Flewelling, Ralph Tyler, 163
Freedom, Rousseau, 73
Freud, Sigmund, 100, 101, 105

Gandhi, 98, 108
Gaunilo, 96
Genetic error, 22, 102, 110
Gestalt, 14, 15, 54
Geulincx, Arnold, 106
Gilson, Étienne, 157
God, 85 ff., 132
  Aquinas, Saint Thomas, 65
  arguments for existence, 92-100
  conceptions of, 86-92
  Nietzschean view, 51-2
  personal, 163-5
  as prime mover, 127-8
  as pure act, 128
  Spinoza's conception, 130-1
Golden Rule, 71
Good, 31 ff.
  indefinability of, 54
Gorgias, 27, 125
  nihilism, 125
  skepticism, 27-8
Government, aristocracy, 61-2, 63-4
  Communism, 78-81
  democracy, 69-72, 73-5
  dictatorship, 68-9, 79, 148
  monarchy, 61-2, 63-4, 76-7
  oligarchy, 62
  polity, 63-4
  princedom, 69
  republican, 59-62, 69

Haeckel, Ernst, 114
Hamlet, 99
Happiness, 33
  Aristotle, 34-5, 63 ff.

Harmony, Preëstablished, 107
Hedonism, Benthamite, 41-3
 Cyrenaic, 37
 Epicureanism, 37-8
 Qualitative, 43-4
 Quantitative, 42
Hedonistic calculus, 42
Hegel, 23, 25, 88, 120, 148
 dialectic, 140-1
 legal philosophy, 75-8
 metaphysics, 128, 140-1
Heidegger, Martin, 23, 26, 114
Henotheism, 87
Heracleitus, 122-3
Herbert, Lord, 89
Hitler, 18, 51, 109, 155
Hobbes, 133, 155
 ethics, 69-72
 political philosophy, 69-72
Hocking, William Ernest, 9, 151
Howison, George H., 163
Humanism, Comte, 153-4
 philosophical, 152
 religious, 90-1
 Schiller, 152
Hume, David, 93, 107-8
 metaphysics, 128, 137-8, 154
 phenomenalism, 166, 167
Hunch, 6
Husserl, Edmund, 165, 167
Huxley, Thomas Henry, 100
Hylozoism, 121

Ideal Utilitarianism, 37
 Moore, 53-6
Idealism, Berkeleyan, 135-7
 Hegelian, 140-1
 Impersonal, 91
 Kantian, 138-40
Personal, 163-5
Platonic, 125-6
Ideas, Platonic, 126, 161
Immoral, 31-2
Immortality, 108-13
 arguments against, 109-11

 arguments for, 111-3
 spurious forms, 108-11
Impersonal Idealism, 91
Instinct, 5-6
Instrumentalism, 150-2
Insufficient evidence, 22
Interactionism, 104, 105
International law, 67-8
International relations, 77-8
Intuition, criterion, 6
 ethical, 45
 Kantian, 45-8
Irrelevance evidence fallacies, 16-8
 ad baculum, 17-8
 ad hominem, 18
 ad ignorantiam, 16
 ad misericordiam, 16-7
 appeal to force, 17-8
 appeal to ignorance, 16
 appeal to pity, 16-7
 irrelevance and, 16

James, William, 23, 25, 98, 113, 120,
 151
Jefferson, 90
Jesus, 51, 98, 108
Jevons, 14
Jung, 105
Justice, Platonic, 59 ff.

Kant, 77, 100, 112, 120
 criterion of morality, 45-6
 ethics, 45-8
 metaphysics, 128, 138-40
Kantian agnosticism, 140
Kierkegaard, Søren, 90, 167 ff.
Kingdom of ends, 47
Knowledge, 33
Knudson, Albert Cornelius, 106,
 163

Labor theory of value, 78, 148, 150
Language, ideal, 154-5
Law, civil, 71-2
 eternal, 67
 Hegel's philosophy, 75

Hobbes, 71-2
international, 67-8
national, 67-8
natural, 66, 70
positive, 67
Legal philosophy, 59-81
Aquinas, Saint Thomas, 65-8
Hegel, 75-8
Lenin, Nicolai, 148
Leibniz, Gottfried Wilhelm, 107
    113-4, 128, 131-3
Leo XIII, Pope, 157
Leucippus, 123, 124
Leviathin, 69-72
Linguistic fallacies, 12-6
    ambiguity, 12-3
    amphibology, 13-4
    composition, 14-5
    division, 15
    emotive language, 12
    equivocation, 13
    figure of speech, 14
    vicious abstraction, 15-6
Linguistic therapy, 155
Locke, John, 128, 133-5
Logic, 1-28
    defined, 3
    relationship to epistemology, 3
Logical Atomism, 155
Logical Positivism, 154-6
Logos, 123
Loyalty, 52-3
    philosophy of, 52-3
    as *summum bonum*, 52
Luther, Martin, 98

Macbeth, 100-1
Machiavelli, 68-9
Macintosh, Douglas Clyde, 111
Majority rule, 7
Malebranche, Nicole, 106
Maritain, Jacques, 157
Marx, 100, 140
    political philosophy, 78-81
    principal ideas, 148
    school of thought, 147-50

Master morality, 50-1
Material fallacies, 11-23
    accident, 18-9
    ad baculum, 17-8
    ad hominem, 18
    ad ignorantiam, 16
    ad misericordiam, 16-7
    ambiguity, 12-3
    amphibology, 13-4
    anthropomorphism, 22
    appeal to force, 17-8
    appeal to ignorance, 16
    appeal to pity, 16-7
    arguing in a circle, 20-1
    begging the question, 20-1
    circle in the proof, 20-1
    circular reasoning, 20-1
    composition, 14-5
    compound questions, 20
    contradictory premises, 23
    contrary to fact conditional, 22-3
    converse fallacy of accident, 19
    dicto simpliciter, 18-9
    division, 15
    emotive language, 12
    equivocation, 13
    false analogy, 22
    false cause, 19
    figure of speech, 14
    genetic error, 22
    insufficient evidence, 22
    irrelevance, 16
    misplaced authority, 21-2
    multiple questions, 20
    naturalistic, 54-5
    non sequitur, 19-20
    pathetic fallacy, 22
    petitio principii, 20-1
    poisoning the wells, 20
    post hoc, 19
    self-contradiction, 23
    tu quoque, 21
Materialism, Dialectical, 80, 148-9
    Historical, 148
Matter, 121 ff., 136, 137, 165
Meliorism, 115

Melissus, 121, 122
Metaphysical Agnosticism, 135
Metaphysical Dualism, 106
  Cartesian, 128-9
Metaphysical Monism, Spinozistic, 130-1
Metaphysical Pluralism, Atomists, 123-5
  Liebniz, 131-3
Neorealist, 161
Metaphysics, 119-43
  Aristotelian, 126-8
  Atomists, 123-5
  Berkeley, 135-7
  branches, 119
  Cartesian, 128-9
  defined, 119
  Eleatic, 121-3
  Hegel, 140-1
  Hume, 137-8
  Kant, 138-40
  Leibniz, 131-3
  Locke, 133-5
  Milesian, 121
  Platonic, 125-6
  Pluralists, 123-5
  pre-Cartesian, 121
  Pythagorean, 124-5
  Schopenhauer, 142-3
Method, analytic, 162
Might, Nietzsche, 50-1
  as right, 50-1
Milesian philosophy, 121
Mill, John Stuart, 14, 43-5, 120
  criterion of morality, 43-4
Mind-body problem, 105-8
Misplaced authority, 21-2, 110 ff.
Moderate Realism, 159
Moderation, in ethics, 35-6
  in politics, 64
Monads, 131
Monarchy, Aristotle, 63-4
  Hegel, 76-7
  Machiavelli, 69
  Plato, 61-2
  Rousseau, 75

Monism, Epistemological, 161
  Metaphysical, 130-1
Monotheism, 88-9, 121
Montague, William Pepperell, 160
Moore, George E., 24
  ethics, 53-5
Moral, definition, 31-2
  principle, 75
  universe, 47-8
Moral argument, 97, 111-2
  for existence of God, 97
  for immortality, 111-2
Moral law, 66
Morality, criterion, 43-4
  master, 50-1
  slave, 50-1
Morgan, C. Lloyd, 95
Moses, 87, 88, 98, 108
Müller, Hans, 87
Multiple questions fallacy, 20

Naive Realism, argument for atheism, 103-4
  as criterion of truth, 7-8
  as a school, 160-1
National law, 67-8, 71-2
Natural law, 66, 70
Natural right, 67, 70
Natural theology, 86, 120
Naturalism, Ethical, 50-2
  Nietzschean, 50-2
Naturalistic fallacy, 54-5
Negative Pragmatism, 9, 151
Neo-Idealism, 167
Neo-Orthodoxy, 167-9
Neorealism, 160-2
Neo-Scholasticism, 156-60
Neo-Thomism, 156-60
  metaphysics, 156-60
  method, 157-8
  political philosophy, 159-60
  social philosophy, 159-60
Nero, 109, 155
Neutral entities, 162
Nietzsche, ethics, 50-2
  master morality, 50

slave morality, 50
superman, 51
Nihilism, 27-8, 135, 140
Gorgias, 27-8, 125
Nirvana, 49, 109, 143
Nonmoral, 31-2
Non sequitur fallacy, 19-20
Noumena, 140

Objectivity of truth, 28
Socrates, 28
Occasionalism, 106
Oligarchy, 62
Ontological Argument, 95-6
Ontology, 120
Optimism, 113-4
Ordination, 65
Organism, state, 75-6
Otto, Max C., 91

Pain, 38
Paine, Thomas, 90
Paley, William, 93, 94-5
Panentheism, 91-2
Panphenomenalism, 107-8
Panpsychism, 92, 131-3
Pantheism, 85, 88, 109, 114, 121,
130
Parmenides, 121, 122
Pathetic fallacy, 22
Peace of soul, 39
Peirce, Charles Sanders, 151, 152-3
Perry, Ralph Barton, 160, 162
Personal Idealism, 163-5
Personalism, 163-5
Personality, 163-4
Persons, 47
Pessimism, 101, 114-5
Schopenhauer, 48-50, 101, 114
Petitio principii fallacy, 20-1
Phenomenalism, 120, 137-8, 166
Phenomenology, 165-7
Philolaus, 124-5
Philosophy, legal, 59-81
of life, 31-55

political, 59-81
of religion, 85-115
social, 59-81
types of, 147-169
of war, 77
Philosophy of religion, 85-115
defined, 85-6
natural theology, 86
relation to science, 85
Philosophy of war, 77
Physical Realism, 160
Physicalism, 155
Plato, 28
Idealism, 125-6, 161, 167
metaphysics, 125-6
political philosophy, 59-62
Realism, 125-6, 161
republic, 59-62
Pluralists, 123-5
Poisoning the wells fallacy, 20
Political philosophy, 59-81
Aristotle, 62-5
Hobbes, 69-72
Machiavelli, 68-9
Marx, 78-81
Plato, 59-62
Rousseau, 73-5
Polity, 63-4
Polytheism, 87, 121
Positive law, 67
Positivism, 120
Classical, 153-4
Logical, 154-6
Post hoc fallacy, 19, 20
Pragmaticism, 152-3
Pragmatism, 25, 120
argument to prove existence of
God, 98
as criterion of truth, 9
principal ideas of, 151
as a school, 150-3
theory of truth, 25, 151
Pragmatists, 120
Predicament, ego-centric, 162
Preëstablished Harmony, 107, 131

Prime Mover, 127-8
Prince, The, 68-9
Princedom, 69
Principle, moral, 75
Problem of evil, 113-5
Problem of truth, 23
Proletariat, 79
Protagoras, 27, 125
Prudence, 38
Psychology, 120
Psychophysical Parallelism, 106-7, 130
Pythagoras, 124-5
Phythagoreans, 124-5

Qualitative Hedonism, 43-4
Quantitative Hedonism, 42

Realism, 156
  Critical, 160, 162-3
  Ethical, 53-5
  Moderate, 156-7, 159
  Naive, 7-8, 103-4, 160-1
  Neorealism, 160-2
  Platonic, 161
  Scholastic, 156-60
  Thomistic, 156-60
Reductionism, 104-5
Relativity of truth, 27, 28
  Protagoras, 27, 28
Religio-Empirical Argument, 98-9
Religion, defined, 85-6
  philosophy of, 85-115
Religious Humanism, 91
Religious Naturalism, 92
Renouvier, Charles Barnard, 163
Republics, Machiavelli, 69
  Plato, 59-62
  Rousseau, 74-5
Revelation, 6-7
Revolution, 79-80, 148, 149-50
Right act, Aristotle, 36-7
  Kant, 45-6
  Mill, 43-4
  Moore, 53-4

Rights, civil, 75
  inalienable, 73-4
  natural, 67, 70
Roman Catholic, 105
  philosophy, 156-60
Rousseau, Jean Jacques, political philosophy, 73-5
Royce, Josiah, 52-3, 88
Russell, Bertrand, 100, 101, 114-5, 147, 155

Salvation, ethical, 49
Sanctions, 42-3, 67
Santayana, George, 100, 160
Sartre, Jean-Paul, 100, 167
Saurezianism, 156
Scheler, Max, 167
Schiller, F. C. S., 151, 152
Scholasticism, 24, 157
  as method of inquiry, 157-8
Schools of philosophy, 147-169
  Analytic Philosophy, 154
  Classical Positivism, 153-4
  Critical Realism, 160, 162-3
  Dialectical Materialism, 147-50
  Existentialism, 167-9
  Instrumentalism, 150, 152
  Logical Positivism, 154-6
  Neo-Orthodoxy, 167
  Neo-Scholasticism, 156-60
  Neo-Thomism, 156-60
  Personalism, 163-5
  Phenomenalism, 166
  Phenomenology, 165-7
  Pragmaticism, 152-3
  Pragmatism, 150-3
Schlick, Moritz, 147, 154
Schopenhauer, 101, 114, 120
  ethics, 48-50
  Idealism, 142-3
  metaphysics, 128, 142-3
  Pessimism, 48-50, 142-3
Schweitzer, Albert, 92
Scientism, 155
Scotism, 156

Self-contradiction, 23
Self-preservation, 70-1
Self-Realization ethics, 33-7
Sellars, Roy Wood, 91, 160
Semantic theory, 26
Serenity, 38 ff.
Sex, 41
Shakespeare, William, 99, 100-1, 108
Skepticism, 27-8, 137-8
   Gorgias, 27-8
   and immortality, 110-1
   of scientists, 110-1
Slave morality, 50-1, 73
Social contract, Hobbes, 70-2
   Sousseau, 73-5
Social ethics, 32
Social philosophy, 59-81
   Aristotle, 62-5
   Hobbes, 69-72
   Machiavelli, 68-9
   Marx, 78-81
   Plato, 59-62
   Rousseau, 73-5
   Thomistic, 159-60
Social reform, Marxist, 80-1
Socrates, 28, 98
   ethics, 32-3
Solipsism, 136-7
Soul, 104-9
Sovereignty, Rousseau, 73-4
Spencer, Herbert, 91, 115
Spinoza, Benedict, 25, 88, 107, 114
   metaphysics, 128, 130-1
Spurious forms of immortality, 108-9
   biological, 109
   impersonal, 109
   social, 108-9
Stalin, 148
State, Hegelian, 75-7
Stern, William, 165
Stoical endurance, 39-40
Stoical resignation, 39-40
Stoicism, 38-41
   composure, 38 ff.
   endurance, 39-40

Epictetus, 38-41
   peace of soul, 39
   resignation, 39-40
   serenity, 38 ff.
   sex, 41
   tranquility, 38 ff.
Subjectivity, 161, 168-9
   as reality, 168-9
   as truth, 168-9
Substance, 130 ff., 134 ff.
Substantialism, 104, 105
Sufficient reason, principle, 132
Suicide, 49
Summum bonum, Aristotle, 34-5
   Bentham, 42, 43
   Epicurus, 38
   loyalty, 52
   Mill, 43
   prudence, 38
   Royce, 52
Superman, 51
Supreme Being, 86 ff.
Sympathy, ethics of, 49-50
Synthesis, 140

Tabula rasa mind, 133-4
Tarski, 24, 26
Teleological Argument, 93-4, 99
Tennant, Frederick Robert, 112
Tennyson, Alfred Lord, 95, 111
Thales, 121
Theism, 89, 100
Theology, 85-6
   natural, 86, 120
   relation to philosophy, 85
Thesis, 140
Thomism, 157-160
Time, 4-5
Timocracy, 62
Tindal, Matthew, 90
Tradition, 4
Tranquility, 38 ff.
Transcendentalism, 140, 167
Transmission theory, 113

Truth, conceptions of, 24-7
  criteria of, 3-11
  defined, 23-4
  of fact, 132
  objectivity of, 28
  Pragmatic theory of, 152
  problem of, 23
  of reason, 132
  relativity of, 27
  as subjectivity, 168-9
Tu quoque fallacy, 21
Types of philosophy, 147-69
  Analytic, 153-4
  Classical Positivism, 153-4
  Critical Realism, 160, 162-3
  Dialectical Materialism, 147-50
  Existentialism, 167-9
  Instrumentalism, 150, 152
  Neo-Orthodoxy, 167-9
  Neorealism, 160-2
  Neo-Scholasticism, 156-60
  Neo-Thomism, 156-60
  Personalism, 163-5
  Phenomenalism, 166
  Phenomenology, 165-7
  Pragmatism, 150-3
Tyranny, 62, 68-9
  Machiavelli, 68-9
  Plato, 62

Unethical, 31
Unmoral, 32
Utilitarianism, Bentham, 41-3
  defined, 41-2
  Ideal, 37
  Miller, 41, 43-5
Utility, defined, 42
Utopia, 59

Value, absolute, 98

  conservation of, 111-2
  labor theory of, 78
  personal, 164-5
  supreme, 98
Verification principle, 156
Vicious abstraction fallacy, 15-6
Violence, 79-80
  Aquinas, 65-6
  Communism, 148, 149-50
  Marx, 79-80, 149-50
  Revolution, 79-80, 149-50
Virtue(s), 33
  Aristotelian, 36
  cardinal, four, 60
  Platonic, 60 ff.
  Plato's definition, 60

War, Hegel's philosophy, 77
Warrior class, 61
Watson, John B., 104
Weltanschauung, 32
Whitehead, Alfred North, 92
Wieman, Henry Nelson, 92
Will, autonomy of, 46-8
  general, 74
  Kant, 46-8
  Rousseau, 74 ff.
  Schopenhauer, 48, 142-3
  Stoical, 40
  unconquerable, 40
Wisdom, 60
Wishful thinking, 110
Wittgenstein, Ludwig, 154, 155
Wolff, Christian, 120

Xenophanes, 102, 121

Zarathustra, 51-2
Zeno of Elea, 121, 122